THE THEODICY
OF THE KABBALAH

The Sefiroth

⊕

ARBRE SEPHIROTIQUE DE BARTOLOCCI.

THE THEODICY
OF THE KABBALAH

The Sefiroth

⊕

Francis Warrain

Translated by
Stephen Churchyard
James R. Wetmore

�֎ Angelico Press

First published in French as
La Théodicée de la Kabbale
Éditions Vega, Paris, 1949
First published in English by Angelico Press, 2024
English translation by Stephen Churchyard
and James Wetmore © Angelico Press, 2024

For information, address:
Angelico Press
169 Monitor St.
Brooklyn, NY 11222
angelicopress.com

ISBN 979-8-89280-043-3 (pb)
ISBN 979-8-89280-050-1 (cloth)
ISBN 979-8-89280-051-8 (ebook)

Cover Design: Michael Schrauzer

TABLE OF CONTENTS

A Note On
Francis Warrain

FRANCIS WARRAIN was born in Marseille on October 10, 1867. His mother died giving birth to him. His father provided him with a deeply Christian education, from which there followed that thirst for the Absolute which oriented his life towards the metaphysical pursuit of the Beautiful and the Good. After his father's death in 1880, Francis Warrain went to live in Paris, completed his high school education, took a degree in law, and prepared for the competitive examination for the *Cour des Comptes*, the French Revenue Service. But he soon saw that this was not the right path for him, and that only the arts, sciences, and philosophy could inspire him. A tireless worker, he became highly cultivated both artistically and scientifically; and when it was necessary for him to begin his career, he chose to be a sculptor. He then attempted, by means of that art, to express his thinking, which had been steeped in musical impressions, particularly those of Wagner's Ring Cycle. He sculpted a figure of Brünnhilde that can be found in the Marseille museum, a Wotan, a

Freya, then a Saint Cecilia and various other works that were exhibited at the *Salon des Artistes français* in Paris. But he remained dissatisfied with his creations.

Here is what he later wrote on this subject, when his book *L'Armature Métaphysique* [The metaphysical framework] was published:

> I met with considerable difficulties in pursuing this vocation. I was a victim of that error which consists in believing that aptitude for execution must go hand in hand with one's ideas. Dreaming of splendid things, I was unaware of what was required to execute them. I discovered that it would always be impossible for me to turn my conceptions into a reality. One thing had struck me: the marvelous rhythmic organization of the works of Antiquity and of the Middle Ages, and the almost total absence of rhythm even in those modern works that in other respects were most remarkable. Now, to my eyes, expressive scope and a speech-like rhythm were what mattered more than anything else, and I could not find a teacher able to show me the way along this path.

He then began to read the works of Jozef Hoene-Wronski and experienced a genuine revelation. Wronski seemed to him to be, along with Plato and Kepler, the only thinker who had grasped metaphysical principles by means of mathematics. Wronski's philosophical system, especially his marvelous "Law of Creation," seemed to Warrain to put in their proper order metaphysical questions that were usually connected in a more or less artificial manner. Warrain thus saw in this work the solution to problems about which the philosophy of his day was in a state of endless disagreement.

The search for the source of the principles of rhythm led him to the study of mathematics, and in particular of metaphysics—of which mathematics is one of the most immediate expressions. He then abandoned sculpture in order to devote himself entirely to metaphysical research.

In the meantime he had written a work on aesthetics, but gave up the idea of publishing it because the books of Séailles, Souriau, and others had in many ways anticipated his findings. He kept only the metaphysical preliminaries to that book, which he published in a small-circulation journal, *La Voie* [The way] (1905), and then collected in a book, *La Synthèse Concrète* [Concrete synthesis], the substance of which was then summarized in his *L'Armature Métaphysique* in connection with the final concurrence of what he called Representative Intuitions, that is, Life.

Warrain had the idea of addressing the problems of mathematical symbolism and continued to publish in *La Voie* a series of articles on non-Euclidean geometries and *n*-dimensional geometries. It was from these studies that his book *L'Espace* [Space] was to emerge.

It was then that he undertook *L'Armature Métaphysique*

(published in 1925). He took four years to write this work, in which he substantiated all his ideas about Wronski's Law. This was the central work of his life. In it, he showed that the three principles of identity, contradiction, and sufficient reason, which when infelicitously treated in isolation produced the diverging perspectives of realism, idealism, and pragmatism, gave rise, when considered together in their necessary mutual dependence, to Reality and Thought. The analysis of the reciprocal reactions between these principles led to the transcendental developments of Thought (law of creation) and explains the transcendental developments of Reality (metaphysical framework), grounded on the Triad and on the Law of Creation.

This "framework" consists of the architectonic of the fundamental conceptions of metaphysics, giving rise to three systems: transcendentals (reality), categories (thought), and representative intuitions (mutual neutralization of thought and reality). The latter are the focus of antinomies, whose progressive resolution culminates in the transcendent synthesis that is the union of reason and life, or the essence of man: and this imposes an anthropomorphic conception of the universe.

As a counterpart to this work, and to take up by the transcendent method the questions addressed in his *L'Armature Métaphysique* by the genetic method, he undertook to work on antinomies. He recognized that the antinomies had to do with man's own constitution in its present state of degradation and regeneration, since they bore precisely on the system of representative intuitions. The four antinomies set out by Kant were only the most obvious ones. As Strada said, every metaphysical problem contains an antinomy. There had to be one in every element of the system of representative intuitions. So he wrote the book, and by in 1911 had only to tackle the antinomy of the "unconditioned," that which concerns the existence and the nature of God.

In the meantime, he began work on the *Theodicy of Kabbalah*, which you have before you, showing the close ties that unite kabbalistic theories with the metaphysical anthropomorphism needed to resolve the antinomies. In 1911 he had also written for the *Annales de philosophie chrétienne* [Annals of Christian philosophy] a study on substance, which he saw as a link between the Absolute and the Relative as concrete unity opposed to the concrete synthesis that is life.

During WWI he was a lieutenant, then a captain, in an Engineers' Battalion. He was awarded the Légion d'Honneur and the Croix de Guerre. Once demobilized, he gave up (because of the sheer extent of the questions to be explained) the idea of writing a work setting out the structure of the antinomies deduced from the Law of Creation, a law with which almost nobody was familiar.

He thought it timely to present (without demonstrating their antinomical character) the most often studied questions that had led him to attempt a metaphysical interpretation of mathematics. Thus ensued the publication of *Quantité, Infini, Continu* [Quantity, infinity, continuum] (1928); *La Matière, l'Énergie* [Matter and energy] (1930); *Essai sur les Principes des Algorithmes primitifs* [Essay on the principles of the primitive algorithms] (1934); *Examen philosophique du Transfini* [Philosophical examination of the transfinite] (1935); and *Éspaces et Géométries* [Spaces and geometries] (1937).

Meta-mathematics fascinated him more and more, for he thought he had found in it the least inadequate analogies, and the most appropriate symbolism, by means of which to order his research, to specify his deductions, and to translate his metaphysical ideas. From the beginning, meta-mathematics appeared to him as a tree with several branches, of which the two most important are Charles Henry's symbolic logic and psychophysics, and Kepler's concepts of harmony. These ideas are dealt with, on the one hand, in *Conception psychologique de la Gamme* [Psychological conception of amplitude] (1921), *La pensée de Charles Henry* [The thought of Charles Henry] (1930), *L'Oeuvre psychobiophysique de Charles Henry* [The psychobiophysics of Charles Henry] (1932); and, on the other hand, in *Essai sur L'Harmonices Mundi de Kepler* [Essay on Kepler's *harmonices mundi*] (1942).

Warrain devoted the final years of his life to the task of making the difficult thought of the Polish master Hoene-Wronski more widely accessible. In 1933 he began publishing *L'Oeuvre philosophique de Hoene Wronski* [The philosophical work of Hoene Wronski], which was to comprise seven volumes. The first volume set out the bases of the doctrine Wronski called "Messianism." The second volume, which appeared in 1936, subtitled *Architectonique de l'univers* [Architectonic of the universe], was wholly devoted to the philosophical canon Wronski called "the creation or genesis of any system of reality." This is the most remarkable part of Wronski's work, the part that gives him a place of his own in the history of philosophy. The third volume (1938), subtitled *Encyclopédie développée d'après la Loi de Création* [Encyclopedia developed in accordance with the law of creation], contained commentaries on topics Wronski had not himself fully explored.

The other volumes of this work remained unpublished because of the war and the author's death. They were to have treated of other matters studied by Wronski, especially mathematics, celestial mechanics, physics, politics, philosophy of history, the creation of man himself, and religion.

Having judged that the doctrines of his epoch were in a state of disorder, Francis Warrain foresaw disorder also in the actuality of worldly facts. The tragic events that turned Europe upside down in 1939 did not surprise him, but the anxiety he felt about them consumed him. Having retired to Val-la-Reine, near Honfleur, in February 1940, he was confined to bed with influenza. From the first onset of his illness, he sensed that his end was near, and faced death with a great loftiness of soul. Pre-occupied until his final breath by the great problems he had throughout his life sought to solve, he died the death of a philosopher and a Christian on February 29, 1940.

Metaphysician and mystic, Francis Warrain devoted his intellectual life to defending and making accessible to modern thought the very specific approaches on the part of the mind that render it possible correctly to resolve the antinomy between the Absolute and the Relative. In the wake of the Pythagoreans and the kabbalists, drawing on numbers and geometry, finding support in the thought of Kepler, Wronski, and Charles Henry, he defined the essential conditions of a gnosis that could mediate between faith and reason, and that can come close to truth.

P. B. M.

Preface

THE ANCIENTS expressed themselves in concrete terms: their knowledge was more intuitive than ours, and they tended immediately towards synthesis, which is the natural goal of thought. Later, however, it was realized that hasty synthesis leads to confusion, and that it needs to be underpinned by prior analysis. Thus was philosophy born, and with it the methodical use of abstract concepts.

The progress of thought consists of gradually establishing the concordance of the profound intuition of the ancients and the precise analysis of the moderns. It is thus a question of discovering a conceptual and abstract equivalent to the concrete terms and images used by ancient doctrines. The attempt at such a transposition in no way supposes that the ancients wanted to disguise an abstract conception under a concrete symbol, nor does it claim to help us discover how the ancients thought about the metaphysical objects of which they speak; it seeks, rather, to discover which abstract notion, conformable to *our* mental habits, corresponds to the object *they* have pointed out.

The image attaches us to concrete reality, but obscures our knowledge of it; the concept enables us to understand it better, but empties it of its plenitude. The union of image and concept will enable us to have a less inadequate idea of these objects, which no image can represent and no concept can define.

A comparison drawn from the scientific field will make clearer what we mean. For the naive person, "boiling" means a sense-perceptible phenomenon: steam, surface bubbles on a liquid, heat, a characteristic noise, etc. For the scientist, it means a transformation of energy defined by certain abstract relationships: temperature, pressure, etc. Does this mean that, in using the word "boiling," the scientifically naive person means to summarize a scientific process? Not at all. The evocation of the simple, sensible fact together with the scientific definition does, however, help us better understand boiling. We say this, not to set our present knowledge against that of the ancients, or science against ignorance, but to highlight the difference in mental attitude towards a given fact. And besides, a scientist who only knows about boiling in terms of energetic theory, without ever having actually seen water boil, will know less about it than the scientifically naive.

Ancient and modern knowledge are opposed to each other rather in the way that descriptive geometry is to mathematical analysis. What the one expresses through drawn lines, the other defines through abstract relationships. There are often two proofs for a single theorem:

one geometric, the other mathematical. Each will be better understood by different individuals, depending on their mental state. But in the field we are proposing to investigate, the difference of mental state will not be that between the common person and the scientist, but that between the different ages of humanity and the different races. For most of our contemporaries, the naive, intuitive approach remains obscure, and only the discursive approach is recognized as clear and distinct, whereas for the ancients the opposite must have been the case.

All this shows that it cannot be a question of restoring the mental state of the ancients. All we can do is bring together, so far as is possible, the resources of the intuitive mode proper to antiquity with the instruments put at our disposal by the discursive mode. The analogical combination thus obtained will elevate our thinking to a more comprehensive and synthetic view of metaphysical realities. But only by reading the texts themselves, and above all by meditating on them, can we come into communion with the ancient doctrines.

It is by reconceiving the text, not by pursuing the literal meaning, that we will acquire this assimilation of thought. Philological interpretations assign words their current meaning, the meaning that corresponds to the objects or phenomena by which ideas are represented. The philosopher, by contrast, is precisely the exceptional being who disentangles the idea from its representation. In his texts, therefore, he uses words to designate what the representation evokes as general, abstract, or limiting concepts. It is through the connections the philosopher establishes between words, then, and not their current usage, that we can enter into his thinking. This is even more true of texts in older languages, where abstract terms are very rare. Consequently, although philology is indispensable for translating a text word-for-word, it is not its role to interpret philosophical writings; it could only distort their meaning.

Finally, it is important not to confuse the interpretation of a doctrine with its historical origin. The genesis of concepts or systems, and their definitive constitution, are two questions that though linked remain clearly distinct. We can push the study of the completed doctrine quite far without worrying about its formation. It is one thing to see how an arch remains standing; it is quite another to know how it was built. The geography of a country does not depend on the path by which we enter it: and if this geography seems to vary depending on the route taken, it is inexact.

Metaphysical notions and relationships are peaks that can be reached by various paths. History shows us the path taken; but the result achieved depends on the path taken only insofar as the goal is missed. A doctrine or philosophical system becomes independent of its historical evolution to the extent that it achieves a clearly intelligible synthesis. It is to explain its obscurities and its inadequacies that we must resort to history. We then discover the causes that led thought away from its goal and hindered the synthesis. Therefore, the more remarkable doctrines or systems are for their scope and soundness, the less their history is necessary to understand them.

We do not in any way claim to diminish the high importance of the history of doctrines and systems, and the precious help it brings us in understanding them: it is only a question of warning against a very widespread prejudice nowadays, which would have the meaning of a doctrine or a system depend on history alone. We have sought to mark the very clear distinction between the study of the evolution of a system and the study of its content; and we wanted to show that the content is independent of historical evolution to the degree it reaches that intelligibility which is the goal of thought.

To study Kabbalah we will have to extract notions that compose it—that is, dissociate an organism whose parts are all intimately intertwined—and this does not happen without mutilation. To analyze such a concrete body of doctrine is always to distort it a little; but to renounce this analysis is to devote oneself to a reverie that effaces its meaning. It is therefore necessary to combine intuitive suggestion with analytical examination; and this is a personal effort that falls to each one of us. Our work therefore does not claim to reveal the rigorous meaning of any arcana; its only aim is to gain well-defined concepts that spare thought from going adrift, and that serve it as benchmarks in its search for truth.

The kabbalistic hypothesis is that Hebrew is the perfect language, taught by God to the first man. This opinion is no longer tenable, but it remains probable that ancient languages stem from a hieratic language composed by those inspired, either consciously or intuitively. Words relating to religion and to metaphysical and cosmological ideas must have been preserved throughout the ancient languages of the sacred scriptures. There must therefore be words expressing the essence of things and their numerical relationships. And the same can be said for the divinatory arts: there is in them a background attesting to a very high metaphysical science.

The speculations of Kabbalah are thus justified in principle. What is defective in them is their uncritical application and the illusory pretension of possessing the pure elements of natural language, when all we possess are scraps and distortions.

Even recognizing this flaw, kabbalistic procedures are nonetheless intellectual ferments that, thanks to the remaining cohesiveness in the languages they work with, can suggest luminous intuitions.

As for the present work, it only has the value of simple research, and I would not like to maintain its conceptions either against an authorized interpretation of Kabbalah, if it exists, or in contradiction with Catholic orthodoxy.

Principles

I. The Notion of God

T O AFFIRM God is at the same time to affirm that he is not something we can conceive; by assigning a nature to him, we destroy the absolute character of our own affirmation. The notion of God therefore entails a fundamental antinomy. Kant exposed this antinomy in all its acuteness; but it has been recognized implicitly by all esoteric doctrines, by Plato, and by St Thomas Aquinas. All the masters have recognized that we have a negative and a positive conception of God. We affirm that God is nothing that we can conceive, and on the other hand that this negation does not indicate a privation of God's being or of his properties, but rather a super-eminence exceeding any notion of being and nature. It is in this sense that we must understand *the nothing, the nothingness, the non-existent* that certain esoteric doctrines have taken as an overarching principle. These terms nevertheless have the weakness of being ambiguous and requiring elucidation. The terms *not-that, ineffable,* are better chosen; and nothing in this regard is more profound than the appellations מה [who?] and מי [what?]—that is, which subject and which object?—that alone indicate God in himself

15

by the double absolute form of interrogation. But by the simple fact that we are led to affirm God, we must admit that he reveals himself through a certain manifestation. Now, what leads us to this affirmation is the whole of reality and the whole of thought: it is therefore by means of the very deepest principles, from which thought and reality simultaneously emerge, that we will characterize in the least imperfect way what God's manifestation is.

The affirmative religious and philosophical doctrines of God have also sought to express the nature of God by means of the plenitude in which thought and reality are identified while yet remaining distinct.

No doctrine leads us as far in this knowledge of God manifested as do the Catholic dogmas of the Trinity, the Incarnation, and the Redemption. But if these dogmas provide us with superior formulas that other doctrines have not been able to achieve, these formulas even so remain transcendent to our discursive reason. Christian theology has clarified the nature of the essential relationships that constitute the three divine hypostases and the conditions in which God enters into relationship with the nature of the world and with that of humanity. And this forms the axis of our theological knowledge.

Kabbalah tends to link the dogmas commented on by Catholic theology with the conditions of human reason. We do not claim that Kabbalah was invented for this purpose, but we do say that it seems to lend itself to this end in a most remarkable way. Several authors, such as

Gichtel, Drach, and more recently de Pauly, have shown the agreement of Kabbalah and Catholic dogmas. Here we only want indicate that Kabbalah is situated as an intermediary gnosis between faith and reason. Apart from dogmas that are objects of faith, affirmative philosophies of God have only sought to construct the positive notion of God through attributes of humanity and of nature brought to boundless perfection. In respect of *act*, for instance, God is designated as first cause and final end, whose existence and perfection are necessary, and whose operation is absolutely free. In respect of the *thought*, God is characterized as being the thought that thinks itself, and that, in this unique thought, contains the thought of everything possible. In respect of *reality*, God is posited as holding, as existence, the integral possibility of categories: we then say that he is infinite, eternal, all-powerful, pure act, universal support and container; that he possesses all qualities; that in him substance is identical with essence. And finally, we say he: (1) transcends any relation, i.e., is *Absolute*; (2) transcends all intelligible relations, i.e., is *Word*; and (3) transcends any synthesis, i.e., is *Life*.

It is more or less to these considerations that the various theodicies come down. They posit the transcendent principle, but they are not concerned to discover how the influence of this transcendent principle comes to be assimilable by created beings, all of whom are subject to the conditions of Relativity. The Absolute, affirmed as such, remains inaccessible; it even seems to deny the possibility of the Relative. Why? Because, if the Relative is outside the Absolute, the latter is no longer absolute, since it does not embrace everything; and if the Relative is comprised within the Absolute, it cannot subsist in relation to it. This leaves us with the serious problem: *How can the Relative exist in the face of the Absolute?* This problem is solved by the introduction of the principle of Relativity into the nature of the Absolute itself. And it is precisely the dogmas of the Trinity, the Incarnation, and the Redemption that establish Relativity (Relationship) within God, as follows:

> The mystery of the *Trinity* reveals that divine unity consists of a trinity of persons determined by relationships of origin.
>
> The mystery of the *Incarnation* reveals how God makes himself a created being.
>
> The mystery of the *Redemption* reveals how God makes the Absolute accessible to the creature.

Now, Kabbalah as a whole seeks to grasp the connection between the divine Absolute and the relativity of the created. Nor is this search in vain, since our reason arrives at the notion of the Absolute and at the idea of God by reflecting on the principles of thought and of reality. The various philosophical systems have limited themselves to representing God through the unfolding of thought and reality; and when they went back to the principles, they were content to posit God as the final term of a process, the stages of which they neglected to examine. Kabbalah, on the contrary, took on the task of discovering the necessary order that, by virtue of the very conditions of thought and reality, establishes the connection between the Absolute and the Relative.

II. Divisions of the Theodicy of Kabbalah

The primary conceptions by which Kabbalah seeks to express the connection between the Absolute and the Relative are: (1) the essential names and the letters that constitute them; (2) the Sefiroth or numbers and the names corresponding to them; (3) the two faces, the persons, and the degrees of the soul and the worlds; (4) the paths, gates, blessings, etc., and the plenitudes developed by the essential names; (5) finally, the names and symbols that express the perfection of the qualities we encounter in creatures, for example: wisdom, the righteous one, Eden and its river, the celestial chariot, etc. Exoteric philosophy, mythology, and hagiography have hardly focused on any but this last order of ideas.

(1) The *essential names* are drawn from revelation. They therefore represent the dogmatic starting point of philosophical reflection. We can say that the essential names Ehiyeh, Yahweh, Yah, Elohim, have for their object limit-notions beyond which the intelligible becomes inaccessi-

ble to us. These limit-notions circumscribe the source of the intelligible relationships that constitute reality and relative thought.

(2) The *Sefiroth* take us into the philosophical domain. We might say they show the Absolute adapting to the conditions of Relativity. Their system expresses the conditions of intelligibility and existence of any non-absolute reality. The Sefiroth mark the emanation by divine thought of the conditions for the possibility of the creation, conservation, and perfection of any reality: they summarize divine thought as it manifests itself through the making of creatures, and as it makes itself known to creatures. We may say, then that the essential names evoke in some way the absolute nature of God. The Sefiroth reveal God as the principle of relativities. The Sefiroth have names also that link the Relative aspect to the Absolute conditions indicated by the essential names.

(3) The two *faces* and the five *persons* of Kabbalah mark also, by degrees, the adaptation of the absolute nature of God to the conditions of Relativity, but under another aspect. The Sefiroth express this adaptation in terms of reason. They derive diversity from unity, and order from the principle of thought.

The two faces mark the two sides of the limit between God as unfathomable by nature, and God as wanting to make himself known. God veils himself, diminishes himself in some way, so as not to annihilate any creature that approaches him. Here, the principle of God's will is sovereign *benevolence*. It is the prerogative of the long face, but it brings on a necessary reaction that maintains the separation between Creator and creature; and this reaction is carried out by the *rigor* in the little face. The two faces express in terms of *act* what the *Ain Sof* and the Sefiroth express in terms of thought.

To the development of the Sefiroth, however, corresponds a hierarchy of persons that expresses the adaptation of the absolute nature of God to the conditions of Relativity as a function of life.

The notion of person in Kabbalah does not, however, have the same meaning as in the Christian Trinity.[1]

Kabbalah recognizes the trinity, which it expresses by the abstract terms "three in one" or "three heads that are only one head" or "three lights that are only one light," whereas in Christian dogma the notion of person expresses relationships of origin. It is from the essential names, then, notably from the tetragrammaton, that we should look for the kabbalistic indication of these relationships.

---

[1] Distinction of persons, relationships, and notions in God (after St Thomas Aquinas, *Compendium Theologiæ*, chapters 60 to 61):

Eodem secundum rem in divinis sunt proprietates et relationes et notiones nisi quod proprietates personales sunt solum 3, relationes 4, notiones 5.

Proprietates personales: Paternitas, Filiatio, Processio.

Relationes: Paternitas, Filiatio (Spiratio), Processio.

Notiones: Innascibilitas, Paternitas, Filiatio (Spiratio), Processio.

Person in the Christian Trinity is taken in the sense of rational support (hypostasis constituted by a conscious subject), whereas in Kabbalah, it seems to us, it should be understood rather in the sense of the Latin word *persona* (mask). The persons of Kabbalah are, in a way, distinct roles played in God's action towards creatures. They mark the degrees by which the Absolute introduces into itself the conditions of Relativity; and this occurs through sexual doubling—considered first in a state of conjunction

---

Relationes in Patre: Paternitas, personam constituens; Spiratio, non constituens sed personæ subsistentiæ inherens;

Proprietates in Patre: Innascibilitas, non procedit ab alio (distinguitur a Filio et Spiritu Sanct); Paternitas. Spiratio.

Proprietates in Filio: Filiatio; Spiratio; Proprietates in Spiritu Sancto: Processio.

Thus, five properties form the notions specifying the distinction between persons; but if by property is meant that which is proper to one alone, only the *relations* allow us to distinguish among the persons, for they are reciprocal; innascibility is the negative of relation.

Paternity and filiation demand two distinct persons.

Innascibility is opposed to filiation, not to paternity; thus, innascibility and paternity can be united in a single person.

Spiration, which is shared by each of the persons, is incompatible neither with paternity, nor with filiation, nor with innascibility.

Procession is opposed to this shared spiration: it requires a third person.

Thus, the five notions are not five subsistents, as are the three persons. Among these notions, only three are constitutive of personhood; the others are inherent to already constituted persons. Innascibility, being a negative property, cannot be constitutive of personhood. Shared spiration presupposes paternity and filiation.

and intimate correlation, then in a state of differentiation and subordination. The queen, the last degree of this hierarchy, is identified with the community of Israel. She is in a way the divine breath vivifying creatures of reason.

As we see, the persons of Kabbalah express in some way the technique, the operational processes, by which God condescends to the creature to elevate it to himself. The Sefiroth illuminate thought from above; the persons envelop creaturely life to uplift and spiritualize it. And just as the Sefiroth correspond to the construction of the human being, so the hierarchy of the persons corresponds to the degrees of unity achievable by the immanent principle of unity in the Relative, that is to say by the soul.

These are the stages that mediate between the Absolute and the Relative. Next come the deductions from these transitional conditions. From the constitution of the tetragrammaton, Kabbalah will draw the hierarchy of the four worlds. As a whole, they will reflect, in the totality of the Relative, the same constitution as that of the Absolute. And this is necessary, because the Relative can only exist to the extent it submits to the same conditions that constitute the principle of all existence, of all intelligibility, and of all possible action.

Then come the combinations of letters, numbers, and figures deduced from the divine names and the distribution of the Sefiroth: they regulate the laws according to which all creation develops. As the most direct derivations of these principles we will have the constitution of the celestial chariot, the eighteen blessings, the thirty-two paths of wisdom, the fifty gates of intelligence, the thirteen paths of mercy, the seventy-two branches, the six hundred and thirteen precepts, and so on. Next will come the plenitudes taken from the essential names; then the combinations of letters and numbers and the biological figures that express the passage from universal and intelligible realities to sense-perceptible realities.

These are the various kinds of conceptions by which Kabbalah attempted to penetrate the sovereign antinomy that arises between the Absolute and the Relative.[2]

---

[2] It seemed necessary to us to present this overview in order to more clearly delimit the object of the Sefiroth. We begin with the Sefiroth, although they logically come after the essential names, because the conception of the Sefiroth is more accessible to our philosophical reflection. It will help us, I hope, to then approach with better results the deeper mysteries of the essential names, to unravel the hierarchy of persons, and to discover the keys to literal and numerical combinations.

The Sefiroth

I. The Nature of the Sefiroth

HE ZOHAR tells us that the Sefiroth are ten forms that God produced "to direct through them the unknown and invisible worlds and the visible ones." And Azriel of Gerona says "they are the power of being of all that is, of all that falls under the concept of number."[1]

The Sefiroth are the veils through which the divine essence reveals itself; they are ten attributes by which God reveals something of his inaccessible essence. According to Herrera, they are spiritual instruments used by their infinite emanator to create, form, and fabricate. "They are not creatures, but notions and rays of the infinite, which by varying degrees descend from the supreme source, without however separating themselves from it."[2] They adhere to the first cause, says Moses of Cordoba, not as to essence, but as to operation; "they are," says Herrera, "the mediators who represent the first cause, entirely occult in itself, who immediately emanate from it, and by the virtue of this first cause produce and govern everything else."

---

[1] See Karppe, *La Kabbale* [The kabbalah].
[2] See the *Gate of Heaven*, in Knorr von Rosenroth's collection.

25

Thus the Sefiroth are not beings, but emanations. They are not divine hypostases, although the first three are often correlated to the three hypostases of the Holy Trinity. Nor are they beings distinct from God and emanated by him—which would lead to polytheism. They constitute the foundation of the world of divine Ideas. They are the ideas by which divine thought makes itself the principle of a possible creation; as such, they are indeed divine emanations, but not emanated beings.

Sefirah (singular), Sefiroth (plural) translates as *numeration* (or simply, *number*). Sometimes the Zohar also calls them *lamps* or *crowns*: "lamp" expresses that they are instruments for the manifestation of light; "crown" is the actual name of the first Sefirah, the one that is the source and synthesis of all the others.

But we must focus on the essential designation: that of *numeration.*

Kabbalah considers that the primordial manifestation of the Absolute in the Relative is based on numbers. Indeed, passage from the Absolute to the Relative implies above all the transition from unity to distinction; and distinction is essentially based on number. Now, it is true that we take note of similarities and dissimilarities among things before grouping them together in order to count them, and that this in fact is the inductive process whereby we pass from the awakening of consciousness to reflective knowledge in the first place. In the metaphysical order, however, number is, rather, an implied condition of comparison as common basis of resemblance and difference.

It should be noted that number is crucial to the distinction of qualities, not as an arithmetic enumeration, but as a metaphysical function, the source of relativity. It is by substituting, for the irreducible fullness of the Absolute, the relationship of the *One* to that which is no longer one—which is to say to the *Other*—that relationship is born. Here already duality and triad appear, because relationship implies both opposition and connection. But this duality and triad do not have an arithmetical character, because the two and three constituting the relationship are such owing to their different roles: objects of different natures are not added together but composed or compounded. The unit, the dyad, and the triad are therefore not 1, 1 + 1, 1 + 1 + 1, but the essential metaphysical modes of all relationships.

We should be able to deduce from these same principles the metaphysical tetrad and the higher numerations. Exoteric philosophy has never dealt with this problem, which seems, however, to have been the fundamental object of Pythagorean teaching. By designating with certain characters the degrees of the relationship between the Absolute and the Relative, and by calling these degrees numerations, Kabbalah suggests to us that the essence of numbers consists of these very characters. And this evokes a most profound metaphysical conception. It would therefore be necessary to analyze the concepts to which these characters correspond, and to investigate whether they correspond to the combination of 4, 5, 6, etc.—these being irreducible, essential, and fundamental terms of all intelligibility. But here we only indicate the problem, whose solution is in turn barely sketched even by Wronski's Law of Creation.

Are the Sefiroth comparable to the transcendentals, to the categories, or, finally, to the metaphysical entities we will call representative intuitions, such as time, space, movement, mind, matter, imagination, energy, evolution, work, value, life? The transcendentals: *being, something, one, good, true*, in a way translate the conditions that underlie the autonomy of being in itself. The categories: *substance, quantity, quality, relation*, etc., express rather the conditions under which existence can be analyzed in terms of intelligible relationships. Put another way, the transcendentals mark a tendency of the intelligence to move from what is relative to the absolute; the categories develop the opposite movement whereby existence submits to the relative, i.e., to that which is the basis of intellectual assimilation. As for representative intuitions, they mark the relationship between the conditions of being and the conditions of knowledge, which constitute the poles of relativity. These three orders of metaphysical ideas correspond to the three abstract points of view that arise from the very constitution of all that is relative.[3] The

---

[3] On this topic see Warrain, *L'Armature Métaphysique*.

Sefiroth on the contrary tend to blend these points of view to transform relation into concrete unity as an image of absoluteness. Also, the names of the Sefiroth are drawn from concepts marking the unifying act: in knowledge, in being, and in their relationship. However, as all discourse is immediately addressed to our thoughts, the knowledge aspect will correspond to the higher Sefiroth, the being aspect will come next, and the operation aspect will appear as the lower resultant of the preceding two.

Thus do the Sefiroth constitute three ternaries: the first made up of crown, wisdom, intelligence; the second of grace, rigor, beauty; the third of victory, honor, foundation; and finally the tenth: kingdom.

The denomination crown embraces three points of view at the same time: it synthesizes the act of thinking by representing the apex of the Sefiroth system with an object that signifies at once supremacy, unity, and totality. The crown intimately unites the points of view of being, knowledge, and their relationship. The Sefirah kingdom marks the receptivity where the three roles of knowledge, being, and the operation that relates them, come together.

Does this mean that, in the divine constitution, the point of view of knowledge prevails over that of being? We will not address here this formidable question, which is, in short, the pivot of Jacob Boehme's doctrine. Let us only say that if the Absolute manifests itself to the relative by way of being, this communication is indescribable, incommunicable, and reserved to those who receive it—and so cannot form the subject of any philosophical development. The fact remains, then, that for all knowledge pursued under the conditions of relativity to which we are subject, it is the principle of the *raison d'être* ("for what reason, to what end?") that constitutes the summit of the intelligible. It is therefore through the function of reason, that is to say through knowledge, that the Absolute must reveal itself as the principle of all manifestation and of all production. We can say, then, that in general the Sefiroth express the concrete act that unifies knowledge and establishes the conditions of thought, that produces being and determines the conditions of reality, and that ensures the emergence, subsistence, and completion of thought and reality within relativity.

These various conditions of the act emanating from the Absolute, to make itself manifest by the relative, through the relative, and with regard to the relative, thus radiate through the numerations or Sefiroth

II. The Upper Sefiroth

Beyond the Sefiroth lies the *En-Sof*, the Absolute insofar as it escapes all conception: it evades all attempts at determination as a Non-Being, understanding by "Non-Being" a supra-plenitude of infinite Being enveloping on all sides the domain of the manifested Absolute. *En-Sof* is therefore not a Sefirah; it is the elusive container of all

Sefiroth and the absolutely occult source of the first Sefirah, *Kether*. And the latter itself is barely conceivable because it is the supreme limit of manifestation and intelligibility.

Kether

The first Sefirah is called the *crown*. It both dominates and embraces all the others. Like all limits, *Kether* can only be conceived in terms of one of the two terms of which it is the boundary. Sometimes it identifies with *En-Sof*, expressing the supreme absence of all determination as an impenetrable essence; other times it is projected into the following Sefirah, *Hokhmah*, to reveal that *En-Sof* is not a lack of being, but the essence of essences: it then marks the supra-plenitude of this absolute that eludes any conceptualization by positing itself beyond the second Sefirah *Hokhmah*, through which it appears. Either way, *Kether* is the threshold between the inconceivability and the manifestation of God. The Zohar sometimes calls it supreme Thought. *Kether* expresses the divine One-All considered in itself (*essentialiter*); the following third Sefiroth *Hokhmah* will manifest God as the *raison d'être* (goal or purpose) of everything (*causaliter*).

The word *crown* expresses by the least imperfect image the character of this supreme limit of thought. The crown is the emblem of royalty, and as such clearly signifies absolute primacy, and superior and irreducible unity. The crown is worn on the head; it is, in a way, the external radiation of the thought hidden under the skull, in the brains. And it to the skull and the brains that, in Kabbalah, the first three Sefiroth correspond. Furthermore, the crown is circular; because it has neither front nor back, neither beginning nor end, it marks the completion and perfection of form. It is the circle that envelops everything. Finally, the crown delimits an empty disk. Its circumference is thus the base of a cone whose apex remains indeterminate on its axis and can be carried up or down to infinity. This highlights the intimate relationship of the crown with the infinite. Its center is elusive, placed on a virtual axis at any distance whatsoever. *Kether* is in a way the *transcendent* and inaccessible state of unity that will become *immanent* in *Malkhuth*. It is the irreducible unity opposed to the synthetic whole.

The Zohar sometimes presents the crown as emanating from the point that represents *En-Sof*, the inconceivable. The point and the crown are both indivisible, indecomposable. But the point expresses this transcendent unity as an irreducible dynamism, and the crown indicates its accomplishment. The crown is empty; yet it contains everything else; and this content remains hidden as in the point. But whereas the point indicates efficient virtuality, the crown marks the supreme final cause, the first cause proceeding from nothing.[4]

---

[4] Sometimes it is said that the crown is composed of seventy-two lights, and this number then corresponds to the name of seventy-two

Hokhmah

This second Sefirah is called *wisdom*. But nothing is more mysterious than this word "wisdom," and it is very difficult to discern in what sense it is used here. The most likely is that the various characters by which we envision wisdom must be fused together to correspond to *Hokhmah*.

The Zohar does not limit wisdom to the Sefirah *Hokhmah*. For example, it says that *Kether* denotes wisdom from above and *Hokhmah* wisdom from below, called eternal wisdom. "*Hokhmah* is the beginning and the end of everything." We would therefore say that *Hokhmah* is wisdom as a principle of creation extracted from *Kether*; and that *Kether* is the essence of the Absolute considered in itself and as the source of all principles. The Zohar seems to suggest that, if the essence of the Absolute is inconceivable, wisdom is the intimate condition that corresponds to that inconceivable essence. And we would be tempted to say of the divine essence: it *is* because it *knows* to perfection how to be.

For the rest of us, wisdom is in a way the selection of the best from among the data of Intelligence; but it presupposes intelligence, and operates within it only by elimination. It is the spontaneous submission of a free-

letters; sometimes it is said that *Kether* has 620 lights, this being the numerical value of the letters that of the letters that make up the word *Kether*, בהר (200 + 400 + 20 = 620). Moreover, there is often talk of 310 worlds: note that 620 is double 310.

dom to a good that dominates it. In God, the order seems quite different: it is, rather, wisdom that in some way precedes intelligence.

Hokhmah thus appears to us as the conceiver that extracts from the Absolute what it wishes to make manifest; and the result of this choice will be the intelligible. Divine wisdom does not *receive* the object of knowledge, it *creates* it.

Thomas Aquinas presents intellect as preceding will. For him, necessary truths are necessary, not because God wills them to be so, but because they are the very consequences of God's nature. For Descartes, on the contrary, necessary truths only derive their necessity from God's will. It seems that the concept of the Sefiroth encompasses and reconciles these two points of view.—It is true to say, with St Thomas, that God cannot make the contradictory exist, because the contradictory is precisely an expression of conditions that deny existence. But God could bring about conditions that remove the contradiction of two things and allow them to coexist. The contradiction is only relative to a domain that is always more or less abstract: it disappears in a more concrete domain. God, then, could cause certain necessary truths to vanish by hiding all the conditions in which they manifest; and he could bring into existence what in the manifested order is contradictory by making the manifestation more concrete. The manifested order is what constitutes the domain of intelligence. We can thus understand that a higher faculty, wisdom, has drawn from the essence of the Absolute (*Kether*) what it wants to make intelligible. Now, given its intimate union with the unfathomable Absolute, wisdom appears as the first principle insofar as that principle is knowable, and therefore as the supreme manifestation of perfection. It is itself the model, the exemplar of the best, and thus eternal wisdom. *Hokhmah* therefore appears as absolute knowledge, eminently spontaneous, the supreme genius that invents and creates the intelligible: it thus makes conceivable what in the essence of the Absolute remains inaccessible to any conception.

Hokhmah could thus be called knowledge as creator of the intelligible—the *conception* that is the principle of all necessary truths. It is a choice, but a choice drawn from the Infinite and the Absolute, and therefore a choice not subordinated to any conditions, but rather a choice that creates conditions by virtue of its intimate union with the Absolute. And these conditions are then the foundations of the necessary truths. One is tempted to say: *Hokhmah* is the science of all sciences, which frames the whole beyond which there is nothing more to know.

Binah (*Tebunah*)

The third Sefirah is *Binah*. In Scholastic Latin this word is translated as *intelligentia, prudentia, informatio*. Note that *Binah* is given as *intelligentia* (intelligence), not *intellectus* (intellect);[5] *prudentia* must be understood in the sense of determination by concentration, by organization;[6] *informatio* adds further detail, indicating that it refers to the construction of *forms*.

This Sefirah, it seems, determines ideas and makes them distinct. As such, *Binah* expresses well the feminine function, the matrix that develops all things. It is Intelligence as turned towards its productions and towards diversity and multiplicity; it is the principle of discursive and distributive intelligence.

If we consider *Binah* no longer in relation to the lower Sefiroth but in relation to *Hokhmah*, it appears as receptive.[7]

---

[5] *Binah* [בינה]: intelligence, judgment, knowledge. *Tebunah* [תבונה]: intelligence, fruit, profit. St Thomas defines *intelligentia* thus: *Actum ipsum intellectus qui est intellegere* (*Summa Theologiæ*, question 79, article 10). Now, for the Scholastics *intellegere* is intuition, vision penetrating the intelligible. In Arabic sources, certain angels are called *intelligentiæ*.

[6] Aristotle considers *prudence* to be responsive to practical reason. It is "the higher principle that thinks of desires under the form of universality, syllogizes them in a way, and coordinates them with a view to the greatest possible enjoyment: this architectonic force of life is prudence." (see Clodius Piat, *Aristotle*, 294).

Prudence is intelligence insofar as it turns to the principles of action: it is only the perfection of the practical function of intelligence (see op. cit., 318)

[7] Between *Hokhmah* and *Binah* there seems to be a relationship similar to that which, in Aristotle, distinguishes between νοῦς ποίητικος (nous poetikos) and νοῦς παθητικος (nous pathetikos). But there is the following difference: among men, the νοῦς παθητικος extracts the diver-

Binah, says Isaac Luria,[8] is represented by two figures. The first, a round figure, is the samekh [ס]; it indicates *Binah* hidden above with wisdom. The second, a square figure, is the closed mem [ם]; it signifies *Binah* abiding over free beings and nurturing them.

This is quite remarkable: the circle expresses unity as fully unfolded to envelop everything; it is unity in the universal; the square expresses differentiation through contrasts, and stability through complementaries.

Hokhmah initiates the first act of thought. *Binah* elaborates and diversifies it to translate it into emanations and creations. *Binah* is, in a way, the Absolute returning towards the relative implied by all created existence. As inherent in the Absolute, *Binah* is *intelligentia*: it understands; as developer of relativity according to Absolute principles, it is *prudentia*.

Also, *Binah* is opposed to matter as is the mother above to the mother below. Intelligence, as receptive to what wisdom has conceived, is in a way like mental matter opposed to the principle of form.

In the Zohar, *Hokhmah* often designates the father, and *Binah* the mother. This agrees with the respective

sity of ideas from the diversity of the sensible and directs them towards mental unity. *Binah*, on the contrary, receives the first act of the conception, and from it draws the diversity that will distinguish the ideas and allow the appearance of the sensible.

[8] See *Commentary on the Siphra Dtzenioutha* in the collection published by Knorr von Rosenroth.

roles we have just assigned to these two Sefiroth in the act of thought. *Hokhmah* projects, *Binah* elaborates.[9] But this correspondence is far from being invariable. Sometimes *Hokhmah* and *Binah* are both called the mother below. Sometimes *Hokhmah* is the mother, and *Binah* the Son of God. Sometimes *Binah* represents the union of the father, the mother, and the son (Idra Zuta). Finally, *Binah* is taken to represent the Holy Spirit, and *Hokhmah* the Word. We limit ourselves to pointing out these relationships, leaving their closer examination to another work.

Da'ath

Da'ath (cognition, science, knowledge).[10] This notion is interposed between *Hokhmah* and *Binah* as being the

---

[9] According to Knorr's *Kabbalah*, the person of the father corresponds to *Hokhmah* in its upper part; it is called Old Man Israel (*Vieillard Israël*) in its lower part. The person of the mother corresponds to *Binah* (intelligence) in its upper part; it is called *Tebunah* (prudence) in its lower part. Should we not understand by *Hokhmah* intellectus, *rational intuition*; and by Old Man Israel the *estimative* lower form of intuition? *Binah* would be the *discursive intelligence* that composes, organizes, and distributes; Tebunah would be the *operation* that discerns by analysis and examination. Compared to the inferior Sefiroth, *Binah* represents the creator as opposed to the product. It corresponds to the term [מִי], Who? *Tzeir* (the group of the six Sefiroth that follow) then corresponds to the term [מִי], What?

[10] *Da'ath* [דאת], knowledge, science, understanding, wisdom, reflection (infinitive of דִעַ, to feel, to apperceive, to apprehend).

result of their intimate union. It is not counted among the Sefiroth because its character is different.

Da'ath is not of the nature of the terms of a relationship, but is itself a relationship. Just as perception is neither in the subject nor in the object, but in the fact of their conjunction; just as action is neither in the agent nor in the patient (that which is acted upon), but in their common operation; just so, *Da'ath* is in some way the fact of the intimate union of wisdom and intelligence in thought.

Sometimes *Da'ath* is located between *Hokhmah* and *Binah*, and sometimes it extends either towards *Kether* or *Yesod*. It constitutes, in a way, a cruciform axis that establishes both a relationship of correlation and a relationship of subordination throughout the whole of the Sefiroth system. For this reason Luria calls *Da'ath* the *influence*. Finally, we could say: *Da'ath* is the root of Relativity drawn from the Absolute.[11]

[11] In the kabbalistic lexicon assembled by Knorr von Rosenroth, it is said that *Da'ath* does not have a vessel like the Sefiroth because it is the *Neschamah*, the *mens* (or mind) of the Sefiroth system. This is the state of *Tikkun* (the restitution). In the previous state, before the "breaking of vessels," *Da'ath* had a vessel, but it did not count as a Sefirah because it constituted the dividing line between the upper three and the lower seven Sefiroth. (See pages 62–66.) *Da'ath* is the middle line, the Vau of the tetragrammaton supporting the two arms, *El* [אל] to the right and *Elohim* [אלהים] to the left. In the *Tikkun* system, *Da'ath* goes from *En-Sof* to *Malkhuth*. It is the Tree of Knowledge.

Hokhmah and *Binah* are, as it were, the two poles of both speculative and practical intelligence. In knowledge, *Hokhmah* stands for the thinking subject; *Binah* for the understanding in which the object of thought is elaborated, and *Da'ath* for the subject's perception of the object. In this operation, *Hokhmah* is the spontaneous action, *Binah* the fixing reaction, *Da'ath* the resulting fact.

Da'ath therefore appears as the relationship in which the two supreme poles of thought—and thereby of all conditions of intelligibility and existence—are neutralized. But at the same time, since *Hokhmah* and *Binah* intimately interpenetrate each other, their own reality is projected above all in their conjunction. And this conjunction is in some way a reflection of their common principle. Indeed, it expresses the very act of *Hokhmah* and *Binah*, and as such, *Da'ath* appears to be the very foundation of the realization of the one and the other.

Da'ath therefore has the dual character of foundation and result. But we cannot consider this in isolation. It is, in a way, the neutral line determined by the opposition of two poles: it connects and separates them at the same time; it results from them while being the very condition of their establishment. The foundational aspect of this dual character causes *Da'ath* to vanish upwards into *Kether*, the supreme and inaccessible principle. But lower down, this dual character will assert itself as a support of the higher, and as the source of lower developments. This explains the affinity *Da'ath* has for the ninth Sefirah, *Yesod* (Foundation), which has just these characteristics.

When the Sefiroth are set in correspondence to the organs of man, *Kether* represents the skull; it is the envelope that hides from us the elaboration of thought. It is supreme thought known only as the supreme reality. Thought and reality are one in the Absolute; but the reality aspect consists in affirming thought as act without revealing its nature. The thought aspect indicates, as a necessary and sufficient reason for reality, the ternary constitution formed by two terms and a relationship.[12] It is this ternary that *Hokhmah*, *Binah*, and *Da'ath* manifest. These three entities make explicit the constitution of the Absolute, which *Kether* represents by a concrete character. Also, *Hokhmah*, *Binah*, and *Da'ath* are called the brains.[13]

III. The Lower Sefiroth

The first three Sefiroth are united in an entirely intimate way and they characterize the very essence of God.

They have also often been made to correspond to the three persons of the Holy Trinity. The following Sefiroth

---

[12] According to Michael of Cordoba, *Kether* represents knowledge or science, *Hokhmah* the knowing subject, *Binah* the known object: and in God these three terms are identified. Karppe disputes this interpretation. Our text shows to what extent we deviate from the opinion of Michael of Cordoba.

more specifically constitute the *emanation*, the irradiation, of the divine essence constructing the world of the divine ideas.

But sometimes these seven Sefiroth are considered an emanation coming from *Hokhmah*, sometimes a synthesis enveloped by *Binah*. And these two points of view complement each other, because *Hokhmah* and *Binah* both intervene in the production of thought—one to conceive it, the other to bring it to life. *Hokhmah* represents the Word more directly; and the Word is the principle of all creation, the beginning and the end. It is the only one of the three hypostases that manifests itself.[14] But *Binah*, which we relate more especially to the Holy Spirit, is the principle of union and distinction, and consequently the support and matrix of all relativity. *Binah*

[13] We do not know precisely how the Zohar intends to divide the centers of nervous activity. Is *Hokhmah* to be understood as the right brain, and *Binah* the left? There would then remain, for *Da'ath*, the cerebellum, the cerebral peduncles, the optic nerves, the striatum, the medulla oblongata, and the spinal cord. It does indeed seem that *Binah* corresponds to the left brain, because according to modern science it is this hemisphere of the brain that appears to be the location of the objects of thought. The role of the right brain is still very poorly understood, and we can wonder if it does not correspond to the subject's intervention in thought. As for *Da'ath*, the Zohar has it circulate throughout the entire body; it would therefore constitute all the nerve centers spread throughout the body and correspond to both the spinal cord and to the major sympathetic nerve centers. However, this interpretation is not the only possible one and the question deserves further study.

[14] See in this sense J. de Pauly's notes on the Zohar, vol. 6, note 831.

will find its reflection, so to speak, in the last Sefirah, *Malkhuth*. This Sefirah designates the Holy Spirit, meaning that it is as important as all nine others put together. In short, the seven lower Sefiroth are the manifestation of *Hokhmah* in *Binah*, which then projects itself into *Malkhuth* to contain everything.

Hesed and Geburah

The fourth Sefirah is *Hesed* or *Gedulah*.[15] *Hesed* is translated as grace, benevolence, sometimes also magnificence. It is therefore the idea of liberality and giving that corresponds to this Sefirah. It comes immediately after intelligence, as being the first fruit of its development. The fifth Sefirah, *Geburah* or *Pahad*, is translated as rigor, power, and fear. It is to this Sefirah that the judgments are attributed. And as has often been noted, these Sefiroth move us from metaphysical notions to moral notions.

But even so, the metaphysical character must persist through all ten Sefiroth. *Hesed* and *Geburah* appear in fact as the immediate derivatives of wisdom and intelligence. They can be translated respectively by the two prerogatives that result from intelligence: on the one hand, the freedom to produce that results from intelli-

---

[15] *Hesed*, חסל: love, kindness, favor, grace, mercy.
Gedulah, גדולה: greatness, magnificence, majesty.
Geburah, גבורה: strength (oak).

gence putting its resources at the service of conceptual understanding and wisdom; on the other, the need for wisdom to conform to everything rational. For us, rational necessity prevails over freedom to conceive because our intelligence is only a reflection of divine intelligence; and for us, wisdom is a choice subordinate to the necessary laws that impose themselves on our reason. In God, on the contrary, rational ideas have their source in his unity and in his life: they become distinct by his choice; and the freedom to conceive and to produce this or that thing prevails over the laws. It is to allow the Relative to assimilate the inexhaustible gifts of the Absolute that separations, restrictions, and rules are necessary. This is the origin of *necessity* and *rigor.*

Considered in the moral world, freedom and necessity become respectively benevolence or grace, and rigor or severity. Rigor results from the very nature of the creature. The creature must be separated from the Creator; otherwise it will vanish, absorbed by the Absolute. But this separation cannot be complete because, for lack of an absolute substratum, Relativity is annihilated. There must therefore be a relative separation and a relative union between the creature and the Creator: it is to these two relationships that the Sefiroth *Geburah* and *Hesed* seem to correspond.

Every created being is composed of existence and quiddity ("whatness"); or put another way, of an element of being and an element of knowing. *It is,* and *it is this or that*: these two conditions are equally essential. But if we say first *it is*, and then *it is such a thing* or *it is in such a manner*, we must not conclude (in line with the Peripatetic philosophy) that *being* is the first condition and that *being such and such* is a condition subordinate to the first. Being appears to us more fundamental than quiddity because it is inaccessible to knowledge, as being opposite to it; but existence can only consist in the affirmation of a manner of being, that is, in a conformation of what *is* to the domain of *knowing*. Now, it is through knowing that beings share something in common, whereas it is through existence that they are separate from each other. We therefore understand that the creature participates in the nature of the Creator through knowing and not through being. It is through the Word, that is to say through the manifestation of God mainly as knowing that the creature is created, that it knows God, and that it can go to him; but it is through its relative being that the creature separates itself from the Creator, who is absolute Being. The Sefiroth *Hesed* and *Geburah* seem to us to correspond to the two most immediate emanations of being and knowing. It is knowing that is productive; being only cooperates in its action; it is knowing that gives; being corners, restricts, limits possibilities to certain effects, having as it does the characteristics of rigor. And if we go further, we will see that *Geburah*, rigor, corresponds to the function of being alone, exclusive of any participation in knowledge—that is, to the principle of rigorous individuation, the principle from which matter emerges. By contrast, *Hesed* corresponds to knowledge emancipated from all conditions, to absolute freedom to invent and produce.

For all things, the Sefirah *Tifereth* will bring about agreement between these two inevitable conditions: separation from the Absolute and participation in the Word.

Hesed is the right arm, *Geburah* the left. It is through the arms that we lift or lower, give or withhold, disperse or distribute.

In the world of the creation (*Briah*), it seems that rigor is prior to clemency; and the Zohar tells us: "the world was created by rigor, but it could not have existed had not clemency intervened." Creation indeed implies a separation, but the creature can only subsist through a subsequent connection with its principle. In the world of formation (*Yetzirah*), by contrast, it seems that the principle of union (*Hesed*) takes precedence over that of separation (*Geburah*). In the world of phenomena (*Assiah*) we would be tempted to place these principles at the same rank and in one accord. But in the world of emanation (*Atziluth*), clemency asserts itself as superior to rigor, because there necessity does not dominate freedom; rather, it proceeds from it.[16]

---

[16] We find in *History of the Jews* a diagram of the Sefiroth where *Geburah* is set as the fourth degree, although on the left, as always.

Tifereth

The sixth Sefirah is called *beauty*; it appears as the liaison of the two preceding Sefiroth: grace or benevolence and rigor or severity. Thus it is named also *mercy* and *heart*. Beauty is made up of a harmony between the rectitude of laws and the gentleness of grace. It is the agreement of the rule with freedom. It is the realization of what, by natural affinity, must be. Thus beauty appears as the central focus of a radiance, that is, as unity and fixity in unconstrained expansion. And from these two characters derive the next two numerations: victory and glory.

As a centralizing focus and projector, *Tifereth* constitutes the heart in the Sefirotic body. Beauty appears as the immanent union of rigor and grace. And this character corresponds to the systematic unity of the Sefiroth considered as the manifestation of the divine essence.

Mercy appears as the transcendent and higher unity that presides over rigor and grace when we consider the Sefirotic whole in relation to the lower worlds. Grace is a spontaneous and immediate gift. Rigor can limit it by rights of law. Mercy frees itself from such rights by a superior will, which gives the gift of a concession and confers on it the value of a right. Thus mercy reconciles rigor and grace in their effects: in this respect it stations itself as transcendent to both. Yet it is not surprising that this same reconciliation, seen in its own domain, no longer appears as the imposed order, but as the innovated order by which the antinomy of freedom and necessity is resolved.

On the one hand, the Sefirah *Tifereth* proceeds directly from the meeting of the three supreme Sefiroth: it represents the content of the crown manifested by the conjunction of wisdom and intelligence. On the other hand, this Sefirah comes sixth as resultant of the two preceding Sefiroth.

From a moral point of view, the heart corresponds to the idea of mercy; from a psychic point of view, it attaches itself to beauty through sensitiveness; from a biological point of view, it represents a centralization is both expansive and attractive.

Tifereth is also called the king or prince of peace. Beauty is indeed a harmonious peace between all the elements combined. It rules and shines like a king towards whom everything converges and to whom everything submits and resorts. The Idra Zuta also compares *Tifereth* to a great tree giving all animals shelter and food.

Netsah and Hod

The seventh Sefirah is called *victory* or *triumph*. It appears as the immediate consequence of the radiance of beauty. The eighth Sefirah[17] is called *glory* or *honor* (Éliphas Lévi says, *eternity*). Between honor and glory is the same difference as between victory and triumph. Vic-

---

[17] *Hod*, הוד: majesty, force, vigor, beauty.

tory and glory are the possession of a good; triumph and honor manifest this possession. Victory and glory both derive from beauty: they express beauty in relation to the regions it rules. Both are distinctly derived from it: for glory can radiate from beauty directly, without needing to assert its power through a victory. Nevertheless, glory has its raison d'être in that it indicates the power to conquer. And thus victory is implicitly given by glory. Victory, on the contrary, does not presuppose glory, but only force. And here we see that absolute force emanates from the mastery that knows how to temper grace with rigor, in the sovereign power of mercy. The supreme force is therefore the one that knows how to give succor and at the same time to be esteemed.

Netsah and *Hod* are often called the pillars or columns of the Temple, Jachin and Boaz, which, according to the works of Knorr, indicate, first, strengthening, and second, vigor (we would say consolidation).

In the body of the Sefirotic man, *Netsah* and *Hod* constitute the thighs. The thighs, like the columns, are supports, but also joints and pivots. Also, it seems we must look to these two Sefiroth for the principles of space and time, creation and progress, action and resistance. The thighs are the first limb joints that support and advance: while one leg carries the body, the other progresses. Victory alternates with the enjoyment of victory, which is glory. Glory spreads when victory is accomplished, not while it is taking place. The Sefirah *Hod*, which expresses the aspirations of the lower towards the higher, corresponds to this celebration of victory, which is honor.

Victory has the character of concentrated unity in a dynamic form: it only separates, breaks, divides for the purpose of submitting diversity to the unity of power. Honor, by contrast, has a more dispersive character: yes, it also is a concentration of the admiration of all towards one, but in this case unity is the result of a competition, and has as its origin a plurality. Victory therefore has an active and male character; honor a passive and female character. These two Sefiroth are opposed to each other like percussion and resonance, like production and propagation. And these will be the two powers as a result of whose concentration the foundation is assured.

Yesod

The ninth Sefirah is called *foundation*. But this foundation is not a basis operating by passive resistance. Rather, it is a dynamic focus that contains the virtuality of all that will unfold to constitute the created world.

This Sefirah corresponds in fact to the male generative organ, which projects into effective realization the seeds of all things. In this same vein, *Yesod* is also called the river coming from Eden, or, again, the Tree of Life. *Yesod* also designates alliance[18] because it is the link between the begetter and the begotten.

---

[18] The French *Alliance* can also mean covenant or wedding ring.

This Sefirah, better than any other, represents the middle column. It supports, in a way, the supreme world, which comes to be condensed within it.

The *righteous one*[19] corresponds to the Sefirah *Yesod*, or rather, to the intimate connection of *Tifereth* and *Yesod*; the righteous one is he whose works are perfectly adapted and consistent with the mission received. *Yesod* is therefore a kind of adjustment or fine-tuning, with a view to a work that is the production of the lower worlds and their orderly attachment to the supreme world.

Yesod, like *Tifereth*, operates the agreement between the two Sefiroth that precede it. But, while in *Tifereth* there is a flourishing synthesis, here there is, rather, a sort of distillation, reduction, concentration, of the energies manifested by *Netsah* and *Hod*, by victory and triumph. Here, victory becomes interior and is transformed into the self-mastery possessed by the righteous; triumph translates into the irreproachable purity of the righteous. After victory (*Netsah*) and glory (*Hod*) comes the righteous one, who takes fair advantage of conquests, and who establishes and assures the alliance of the king with his kingdom.

Malkhuth

The tenth Sefirah is called *kingdom* or *reign*, and often also *basis* and *corolla*. It completes the Sefiroth system. In

---

[19] Or, the just (*Le Juste*).

turn, it envelops the world below, in which the ten Sefiroth will project their branches and establish their hierarchy: an essential condition for any system of realities. *Malkhuth* is therefore in a sense outside the system it completes: it is its reflection. Note also that when we represent the Sefiroth system by the human being, *Malkhuth* is under his feet.

Malkhuth is called by the Zohar the *holy of holies*: a feminine, mysterious, and hidden region. *Malkhuth* is a sort of lesser image of *Kether*. *Kether* envelops the entire Sefiroth system in an intimate unity we cannot even imagine. We are therefore reduced to considering it as the *raison d'être* from which the other Sefiroth proceed. And although all these Sefiroth return the crown, or rather do not leave it, their process must end with a new and explicit aspect of the One-All implicitly revealed by the crown. But by the very fact that this content has become explicit, it has somehow come down to adapt to our understanding. It therefore appears in a somewhat passive, feminine form, which allows itself to be touched by us, and which feeds our intelligence and our life. In a sense, it is God revealing himself through his created work and appearing through it. It is this revelation of God through his work that pantheists mistake to be God himself.

In summary, *Malkhuth* seems to express the presence of God in this world and his preserving, regulating, and animating action; and in particular, his providence. Nevertheless, *Malkhuth*'s "low station" (*inferiorité*) is in a sense only a condescension, for this Sefirah expresses the synthesis of all the others. As such, according to de Pauly, it designates the Holy Spirit, and is as important as the nine other Sefiroth together.[20]

IV. The Divine Names Corresponding to the Sefiroth

The divine names are of three kinds. The most numerous are simple epithets: they indicate divine intervention in the order of created things, through a relative quality that is supposedly perfect. It is in this sense that we will call God the Most High.

The other names, much rarer, designate the divine nature by means of concepts that, for our reason, correspond to the first principles. There are, however, several, because we can only express the absolute Principle by means of denominations that are complementary to each other; our reason evokes the concept of the Absolute, but can only retain it as an object of thought by imbuing itself with relativity. By this very fact, the names that express the divine essence translate, in some way, the limiting state where the constitution of the Absolute is covered with the veil of relations so as to become accessible to our thinking.

---

[20] See de Pauly's translation of the Zohar, volume 6, note 1189.

53

Now, the Sefiroth and the procession of the persons (of Kabbalah) express the adaptation of the Absolute to Relativity, and show it in a double aspect.

Emanation, which is the essence of relativity, will be described by the Sefiroth and figured by the five persons; the emanator that is the essence of the Absolute will be indicated by the divine names.

As we have seen, the persons mark the essence of Relativity establishing itself in the very heart of God. The essence of the Absolute expressed through the persons will be given by the name that explicates the divine essence, that is to say the tetragrammaton. The four letters of the name mark the correspondences of the absolute functions associated with the divine relations that constitute the persons. In due course, the other names will come to be applied to the persons according to the characters they highlight.

The Sefiroth mark the essence of Relativity projecting itself, as it were, outside of God to serve as conditions for creation and evolution. In each Sefirah, the Absolute will be designated by the subjective character of which it constitutes the objective manifestation—hence the divine names applied to each Sefirah, names holding the middle ground between names that signify (in a more or less direct way) the divine essence and epithets (i.e., appellations that signal God by a quality of relative nature, considered in its fullness).

The Sefiroth articulate the intelligible generated by the

act of the absolute; the corresponding divine names indicate the modes of action, the radiance of which constitutes the Sefiroth.

But the essential names will be found in the supreme Sefiroth because they are more intimately linked to the very essence of God. And the tetragrammaton develops throughout the entire Sefiroth system because the Sefiroth are made in the image of God. Moreover, this name (the tetragrammaton) is situated on the Sefiroth that correspond most directly to the explicit, unitary manifestation that affirms itself through the essence of the relative, that is to say on the Sefiroth *Hokhmah* and *Tifereth*.

The correspondence of the divine names to the Sefiroth has some variations:

Kether	Ehiyeh
Hokhmah	Yah *or* Yahweh
Binah	Elohim *or* Yahweh-Elohim [Adonai (*Kircher*)]
Hesed or *Gedulah*	El
Geburah or *Pasad*	Elohim Gibor [Shaddai (*Philip of Aquino*)]
Tifereth	Eloha *or* Yahweh
Netsah	Yahweh-Sabaoth
Hod	Elohim-Sabaoth
Yesod	Shaddai *or* El-Hai
Malkhuth	Adonai [Yah (*Lenain*)]

(Exceptional variants in square brackets, with authors who report them; frequent variants linked with conjunction *or*.)

55

Ehiyeh. The name Ehiyeh is translated: *I am* (Sum qui sum) as opposed to Yahweh, which is translated: *He is.* The name Ehiyeh therefore invariably corresponds to *Kether.* It is the name that seems to express God knowing himself prior to any manifestation.

Yahweh. By contrast, the name Yahweh (the tetragrammaton) seems to express the divine essence making itself intelligible to the rational creature: the divine essence as the raison d'être of everything conceivable. Thus, this name is applied sometimes to *Hokhmah,* expressing the intelligibility of the divine essence; sometimes to *Tifereth,* which is as it were the full manifestation of the divine essence hidden in *Kether.* The tetragrammaton can therefore be applied to both Sefiroth. When Yahweh is associated with *Hokhmah,* it is the name of Elohim that is applied to *Binah* and often preceded by the name Yahweh.

Elohim. According to the analysis made by the Zohar and the commentators, Elohim appears to designate God as the efficient cause. It marks the union of God with created nature. And this name corresponds well to *Binah,* which elaborates the intelligible and introduces the relationships of distinction and connection, that is to say the conditions of all non-absolute existence. We often unite the two names Yahweh and Elohim on the Sefirah *Binah* to indicate that Yahweh and Elohim are only the same essence considered under two different aspects. We would be tempted to say: Yahweh expresses the transcendence of God; Elohim indicates God's immanent intervention within Relativity. Elohim is sometimes a proper name, sometimes an attribute—which is understandable, since this name indicates God's connection with nature. It is located especially on *Binah*, which marks the germination of Relativity, and envelops the lower Sefiroth at the same time as it closes the upper ternary on itself.

Yah. Often, it is the name Yah that is applied to the Sefirah *Hokhmah*: the name Yahweh is then transferred either to *Binah*, or rather to *Tifereth*. The name Yah, composed of the two first letters of the tetragrammaton, seems to indicate the immediate and indissoluble procession that takes place between the incommunicable essence of God and its manifestation. It is often interpreted as marking the procession from the Father to the Son, the third Sefirah corresponding to the Holy Spirit. But we will not dwell on the problems raised by these fundamental names and their correspondences with the divine persons. Here we must limit ourselves to considering their connection with the Sefiroth.

El. The name El is universally attributed to the Sefirah *Hesed*. El means greatness, strength, elevation, and it is at first surprising to see it applied to the Sefirah of grace, mercy, freedom. But in fact, grace marks a degree of freedom greater than rigor and justice: giving freely assumes more power than paying fairly. The name El seems to express God above all law.

Elohim Gibor. To *Geburah* is generally applied the name Elohim Gibor (robust Elohim). We see here force considered as the more or less inflexible power of the law.[21] Philip of Aquino applies here the name Shaddai (sufficient), undoubtedly to affirm the restrictive character to which the Sefirah of rigor or fear corresponds.

Eloha. When the name Yahweh is not applied to the Sefirah *Tifereth*, it corresponds to the name Eloha. This name is given as indicating the union of the male principle and the female principle. According to Philip of Aquino, it is the singular of the name Elohim. The plurality and inconsistency of Relativity expressed by the word [מי], which means sea, is replaced by the [ו]. This name seems to mark the return of efficient causality to the final cause—by the synthesis of the two complementary principles. This indeed is the role of the Sefirah *Tifereth*, which marks the fullness of the divine manifestation. It is also because of this fullness that we apply the tetragrammaton to *Tifereth*. It seems that the name Yahweh placed here expresses the direct manifestation of the essence hidden in *Kether*. The name Eloha would mark

---

[21] As for the name Elohim, it will be found in the two Sefiroth that are on the side of *Binah*, i.e., on the side of the Sefiroth that have the distributive character.

this manifestation as a return to the supreme goal of existence through the full accomplishment of causality and of finality.

Yahweh-Sabaoth / Elohim-Sabaoth. To the names Yahweh-Sabaoth and Elohim-Sabaoth correspond, respectively, the Sefiroth *Netsah* and *Hod.* These two Sefiroth correspond in some way to dynamic and static intervention. Hence the name Sabaoth (armies, hosts). Victory has a dynamic and unitary character; and it associates with Sabaoth the name Elohim as characteristic of the own essence of God. Honor associates Sabaoth with the name Elohim, as characteristic of God emanating the principles of Relativity.

Shaddai. To *Yesod* we apply either the name Shaddai (sufficient, almighty) or the name El-Hai (Living God). One of these names explains the other; that is, what is almighty is sufficient: and only life draws power from itself and identifies with the sufficient reason for its existence. Life brings together in itself the efficient cause and finality: it closes the cycle of Raison d'Être. And these characters correspond well to the Sefirah *Yesod*, in which the energies developed by the hosts or armies are condensed in some way to this Sefirah, which is the foundation, the source of all production.

Adonai. Finally, the name Adonai corresponds to *Malkhuth* (lord)—that is, God in his sovereignty over the world.

As we see, the divine names corresponding to the lower Sefiroth often have in some way a double aspect. At first glance, they seem to express simple attributes: Great God, Strong God, God of Hosts, Living God, the Sufficing, the Almighty, the Lord. But at the same time, in a so to speak immediate way, these simple attributes imply metaphysical characteristics derived in essence from the notion of the Absolute: freedom, necessity, projection and aspiration, sufficient reason, life and possession.

The System
of the Balance

I. Fundamental Relationships

E HAVE just reviewed all the distinct modes that, according to Kabbalah, express the adaptation of the Absolute to the conditions of Relativity as a function of reason. And these modes are the Sefiroth. It remains to be seen how these modes are distributed and interlinked to fulfill this role of mediating terms. It is therefore necessary to examine the combination of the Sefiroth into a system.

First of all, we consider each Sefirah as enveloping all those inferior to it, and as enveloped in turn by all those superior to it. This notion is the first that presents itself when we oppose an effect to its total cause. The cause, in this case, necessarily takes precedence over the effect, which it envelops if the effect does not exhaust the cause. This is the first relationship between the Absolute and the Relative.

But this primordial relation is only the seedling of a system, the virtuality of an unfolding still held in reserve in its principle. From there, the thought moves to a second notion, that of subordination. The effect is then conceived as detached from the cause: it has its own existence but is connected to the cause by a link of dependence. The relation of subordination transforms what initially was *envelopment* into *submission*. And this is represented by a graduated linear distribution.

This distribution corresponds to the time of the kings of Edom, kings who were unable to survive, except the last one. The three first Sefiroth have remained intimately united, because they represent the very structure of the Absolute as concrete. From this structure comes the Principle of all Relation. If there is a descending procession from *Kether* to *Binah*, there is in some sense a perfect reflection from *Binah* towards *Kether*. In this way, subordination resolves into an intimate union from which the correlation of *Hokhmah* and *Binah* will emerge.

But the seven lower Sefiroth are only derivative emanations, a descent into the Relative; they are not constitutive, only emanated. But the relationship of Absolute to Relative is transcendent and incommensurable. With regard to the Absolute, the Relative is like nothingness. By its very condition, it cannot oppose itself as the term of a relationship with the Absolute. This results in the death of the kings of Edom, or, which amounts to the same thing, the "breaking of the vessels." (Genesis 36:31–39)

Does this world of the kings of Edom really indicate an historical era? Is there any connection between this destruction and the fall of the bad angels? How should we interpret this production, which looks to have been a failure? We will not attempt to answer these questions.[1]

Still, this breaking of the vessels expresses the antinomy inevitably raised by the relationship of the Relative and the Absolute. Indeed, the Absolute seems to exclude everything that is not reduced to it; and the Relative can only conceive the Absolute by making it Relative. The vessels sought to embrace the Absolute, and they were broken. The last one, however, instead of breaking, underwent a deformation that brought it to a state of chaos. And it is this chaos that will in some way be the fulcrum, the germ, of regeneration.

The breaking of the vessels also expresses a fundamental idea: for the Relative to be, it had in a certain way to be separated from the Absolute. No separation, no Creation: this is a primordial condition, necessary but not suffi-

---

[1] "This idea of the breaking of the vessels was developed by Luria from a suggestion made in the Zohar, where mention is made of the destruction of worlds in which only the forces of *Geburah*, the Sefirah of stern judgment, were active, and which were therefore destroyed by this excess of sternness. This event in turn is placed in relation to the list of the kings of Edom in chapter 36 of Genesis, of whom nothing is said but that they built a town and died. 'And these are the Kings that reigned in the land of Edom'—Edom signifying the realm of stern judgment untempered by compassion. But the world is maintained only through the harmony of grace and strict judgment, of the masculine and the feminine, a harmony the Zohar calls the Balance. The death of the "primordial kings" thus reappears in Luria's system as the breaking of the vessels." G. Scholem, *Major Trends in Jewish Mysticism*, lecture 7.

cient. The breaking of the six vessels corresponding to the Sefiroth *Hesed*, *Geburah*, *Tifereth*, *Netsah*, *Hod*, and *Yesod*, and the reduction of *Malkhuth* to chaos, seem to represent matter with its dual functions. The "shells" coming from the breaking of the vessels would correspond to the arresting function ("bringing to a stop"); the state of chaotic deformation of *Malkhuth* would correspond to the malleability function ("plasticity"). Through its arresting function, matter resists spiritual penetration, hence the "shells"; through its malleability function, matter submits to the spirit by receiving form; and this corresponds well to the idea of basis to which *Malkhuth* corresponds.[2]

The restitution of the vessels produced the current distribution of Sefiroth, the one we will be analyzing. It is carried out by the principles of male and female disposed face-to-face, and by the regime of the Balance; it proceeds by elevation from the lower to the higher, i.e., by

---

[2] "For Luria, the deepest roots of the 'shells'—the forces of evil— existed already before the breaking of the vessels were mixed up, so to speak, with the lights of the Sefiroth and the residue of *En-Sof* in the primordial space. . . . Not from the fragments of the broken vessels but from the 'dross of the primordial kings' did the domain of the *Kelipah* or 'shells' arise. . . . The Zohar's organological imagery is developed to its logical conclusion: the breaking of the vessels is compared to the 'breaking through' of birth . . . also accompanied by the externalization of what might be described as waste products. In this manner, the mystical 'death of the primordial kings' is transformed into the far more plausible symbol of a mystical 'birth' of the pure new vessels." Ibid.

evolution. But this evolution is consolidated by a descent of higher principles that establish themselves like an unshakable framework supporting everything, and envelop themselves in lower principles in order to attenuate the energy of their radiation.

We therefore see the antinomy resolved by a new process: the Absolute incarnates itself in some way in the Relative, cloaks itself therein and penetrates it, enlivening it. Here the relationship of transcendence between the Absolute and the Relative changes into one of immanence. But this transformation raises a further antinomy, because the Absolute cannot lose its nature: it cannot become in some way interdependent with the Relative and enter into an alliance with it. The solution to this antinomy is given in a marvelous way by the celestial man, Adam Kadmon, a notion that seems to correspond on the metaphysical level to the conception of Christ.

Man's essence can be defined as *rational living being*. But life is that which is its own principle and end: it is the autonomy of reality. Reason is what establishes all relationships and accounts for them: it is the autonomy of thought. Both mark the function of the Absolute making itself immanent in Relativity, because life and thought both consist only of relations.

The Absolute therefore splits in some way to communicate itself to Relativity; but Relativity must be brought back to the Absolute by the union of these two functions of the Absolute insofar as it has become immanent in the

Relative: life and reason must become one. This is the state of perfection that defines the essence of man; a state realized by the Absolute in the person of Christ, or the *Adam Kadmon*, and which is goal towards which all men strive.[3]

We will not probe here into the supreme problem of the intimate penetration of the Absolute and the relative through the divine man. This would lead us to address the very difficult question of the persons and the history of the restitution that followed the breaking of the vessels. What must be remembered here is that the Sefiroth system will be distributed according to the pattern or plan of man. Now, man is first of all a thinking and living organism, that is to say a whole in which the unity of consciousness and life intimately penetrates all the parts and all the varied functions, due to the multiplicity and

[3] "In the stage corresponding to the manifestation of God under the aspect of *Adam Kadmon*, before the breaking of the vessels, the forces in action are not yet altogether parts of an organic whole, and likewise have not yet assumed a distinctive, personal, and characteristic configuration. Now that the vessels are broken, a new stream of light wells from the original source of *En-Sof* and, bursting forth from the forehead of *Adam Kadmon*, gives a new direction to the disordered elements. . . . Every Sefirah is transformed from a general attribute of God into what the Kabbalists call a *Partsuf* [persona] of God. . . . The God who manifests himself at the end of the process represents a great deal more than the hidden *En-Sof*. He is now the living God of religion . . . a new conception of the personal God." Ibid.

diversity that constitutes the Relative. The system of the Sefiroth will therefore be such that all its parts will be connected by channels, and that in each of them the entire system will be reflected. Secondly, man appears as the instrument that connects the Absolute and the Relative; and this function is represented by its main organs: head, heart, genitals, and limbs. These organs manifest the connection of the Relative to the Absolute through thought, life, generation, distribution (arms), movement (legs), and lastly, support on the creation (feet). Finally, man is built according to a shifting or mobile equilibrium with a tendency to momentary asymmetry: and here we come back to the regime of the Balance mentioned earlier.

It is the structure of the Balance that we are mainly concerned with here. In its simplest state, a balance includes a fixed axis (middle column, generally vertical), a beam forming a T or cross with this axis, and two scales (pans) suspended at either end of the beam.

The Balance gives rise to three fundamental relationships: (1) the equilibrium between the scales establishes a relationship of *correlation*; (2) the common suspension of the scales at a point of support, and the support of the entire system, evoke a relationship of *subordination*; (3) the different roles of the two scales in the weighing introduces a *differentiation* between the opposing terms, generating an orientation, current, or flow.

In what follows, we will be referring to Athanasius

Kircher's model because it appears to correspond faithfully to the doctrine of the Zohar and the Idra,[4] while also making up for some insufficiencies to be found in the indications provided by these texts.

II. Bilateral Equilibrium

We see right away that the Balance establishes the ternary and the quaternary. The relationship of opposites to the connection between them brings the ternary, but it also brings the quaternary, because the connection between opposites is *itself* based on the principle that prevails over, penetrates, and supports the whole.

We will therefore have a higher ternary where unity reveals itself as the source from which duality issues: i.e., there will be a convergence of *Hokhmah* and *Binah* towards a higher term, *Kether* (see figure I). Here the opposition is still enveloped in union. Duality therefore has the character of a relationship of complementaries.

---

[4] There are two texts in Zoharic literature called Idra: the Idra Rabba and the Idra Zuta. The Idra Zuta (Small Assembly) serves as a continuation of the Idra Rabba (Greater Assembly), at which Rabbi Shimon bar Yochai first revealed mystical secrets to his followers. Three participants did not survive that ecstatic experience, so when the Rabbi Shimon reconvened the group on the day of his death, it was smaller (hence the name "Small Assembly"). Idra Zuta describes Rabbi Shimon joyously sharing mystical secrets he had previously withheld, in order to pass into the next world "unashamed." ED

This ternary, where unity so to speak envelops duality, must correspond to the manifestation of an explicit opposition having been brought back to unity by synthesis. The opposition concerned is asserted by *Hesed* and *Geburah* as antagonism; the synthesis is achieved through *Tifereth* (see figure II). It is like a contention brought to closure through the central term.

Tifereth is the manifestation of the unity emanating from *Kether*: i.e., between these two Sefiroth there is direct communication. By contrast, *Hesed* and *Geburah*, emphasizing accentuated opposition, stem from the principles of opposition directly—the one from *Binah*, the other from *Hokhmah*. There is no channel running from *Binah* to *Hesed*, nor is there one running from *Hokhmah* to *Geburah*. On the other hand, *Hesed* and *Geburah* are linked together like *Binah* and *Hokhmah*. But whereas the channel interposed between *Hokhmah* and *Binah* will mark their distinction within an intimate coupling, that connecting *Hesed* and *Geburah* will moderate the antagonism that would disrupt the equilibrium entirely were it to become absolute.

Finally, *Tifereth* communicates with both *Hokhmah* and *Binah* directly. In other words, manifestation in all its fullness can be derived immediately from the duality of complementaries without passing through the phase of antagonism. But this fullness, sufficient for the Absolute itself, is not sufficient for adaptation to the Relative. For this, it was necessary to establish antagonists to provide

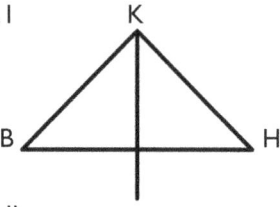

Fig. I

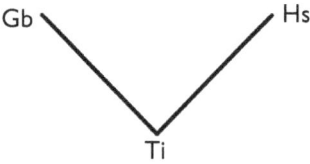

Fig. II

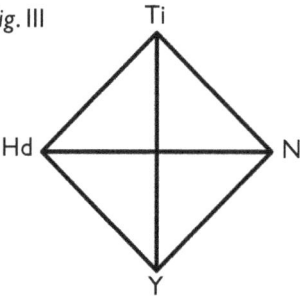

Fig. III

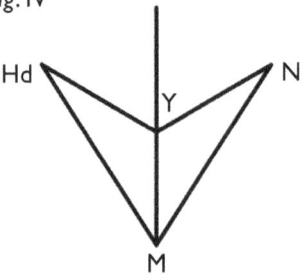

Fig. IV

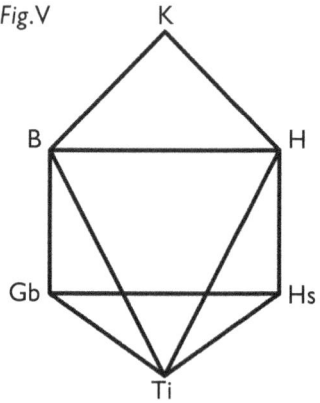

Fig. V

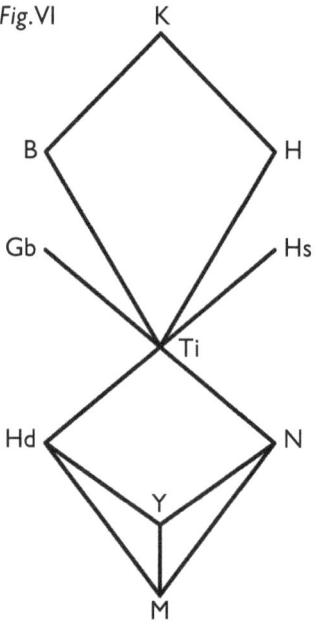

Fig. VI

K: *Kether*; B: *Binah*; H: *Hokhmah*; Gb: *Geburah*; Hs: *Hesed*;
Ti: *Tifereth*; Hd: *Hod*; N: *Netsah*; Y: *Yesod*; M: *Malkhuth*

the function of separation without which the Relative never has its own existence and cannot remain distinct. On the other hand, if this antagonism remained such, it would prevent the Relative from achieving the concrete unity without which it cannot exist. The antagonism must therefore result in a synthesis, which is *Tifereth* (see figure III). *Tifereth* does not cancel the antagonism, but reconciles it. And then the fullness of the Absolute is not only developed (the convergence of *Kether*, *Hokhmah*, and *Binah* was sufficient for this), but is also explained. It embraces in all their amplitude the dissolving conditions of the Relative; and it knows how to accomplish the sovereign, perfectly-defined One-All, while satisfying and overcoming the extreme tendencies that oppose concrete unity with boundless diffusion (*Hesed*) and inflexible restriction (*Geburah*).

Tifereth is immediately connected to each of the Sefiroth, excepting *Malkhuth*. It is the supreme solution to the essential antinomy that arises from the relationship between the Absolute and the Relative.

But the manifestation of the Absolute in *Tifereth* cannot be a simple reflecting of the Absolute upon itself. The senary[5] that leads to this Sefirah marks the manifestation of the Absolute in a perfect relationship. And by the very

---

[5] Senary: the number six; a set or sequence of six things; in the seventeenth century, often, the six days of the creation. Thus, similarly, quinary (5), septenary (7), denary (10), etc.

71

fact that the essence of the relationship is accomplished in all its fullness, it identifies the Absolute and the Relative. This perfect relationship of which *Tifereth* expresses the integration reveals itself as being the essential form by means of which the Absolute is fully explained. Absoluteness and Relation are there as the two aspects, occult and manifested, of the same supreme reality, which is the supreme thought itself. This senary completely fulfills all the conditions of a conceivable Relativity; but by this very fact it no longer corresponds to the production of existences maintained under the conditions of Relativity—because this perfect accomplishment identifies the Relative with the Absolute.

The Relative can only be relative if it remains relatively accomplished; it can never be complete in itself. It is therefore necessary for the supreme Principle to draw from the relationship of the Absolute to the Relative a new function that establishes Relativity as dependent on the Absolute. This will result in fecundity and the union of the higher with the lower. The system must therefore end in a sort of suspension, and with an axial extension establishing the penetration of the supreme Principle right to the limits of Relativity.

The fullness of manifestation, *Tifereth*, will therefore become principle in turn; it will project a duality, a mixture of the two previous ones, a duality that will participate in coupling (conjunction) and disjunction, that will have the character of a transition, and that will be the principle of action and movement. The two Sefiroth *Net-sah*[6] and *Hod* have these characters: they correspond to the notion of Sabaoth or armies (hosts). But this third group, by virtue of its transitive character, must present the opposition of cause and end. The cause appears as a projection, the end as a result. Also, we have a quaternary arrangement formed by *Tifereth* as origin, *Yesod* as result, *Netsah* and *Hod* as concurrent conditions (see figure IV).

[6] In the interpretation by Stanislas de Guaita of one of Heinrich Khunrath's diagrams (reported by Papus in his *Traité de Science occulte* and in the metallic Sefiroth described by Éliphas Lévi), the Sefirah *Netsah*, although coming seventh, is found on the left, the female side. This appears to contradict the Zohar, which allocates to *Netsah* the right thigh and to *Hod* the left. This arrangement breaks the alternation of the sides in the distribution of Sefiroth regulated by the system of Balance, as we will later see. What can explain this variant, however, is the transitional character these Sefiroth establish between separation and reunion. Victory brings unity into multiplicity. Glory builds unity by filling diversity.

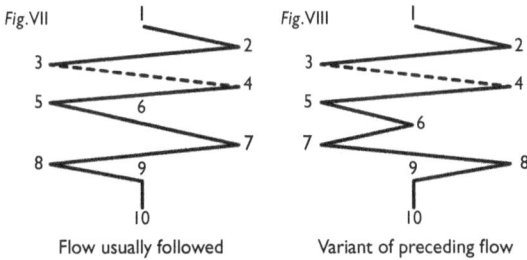

Fig.VII — Flow usually followed
Fig.VIII — Variant of preceding flow

The point of arrival of these two Sefiroth therefore has an opposite character to their point of departure. Nevertheless, it seems that, for the world of emanation at least, the principle takes precedence over the result, and consequently that we must adhere to the usual distribution: *Netsah* on the right, *Hod* on the left.

This quaternary is therefore a reduction of the upper senary, obtained by the transitive character of *Netsah* and of *Hod*. *Yesod* therefore opposes *Tifereth* in like manner as the determination of action opposes the perfection of the state. This determination must correspond to perfect action; it therefore opposes to fullness the character of *sufficiency* and the *omnipotence* to produce. *Yesod* therefore shows us the principle of action as resulting from the transition between the duality of complementaries and the duality of antagonists.

Through *Yesod*, the Absolute finds itself in some way adapted to the condition of the Relative, so as to make immanent in the Relative the function of the Absolute as the *foundation* implied by all relationships. But *Yesod* is the Absolute concealed within the Relative; its omnipotence will be revealed by penetration; and this will bring about to the burgeoning of Relativity as a synthetic and organized whole: *Malkhuth*, the kingdom, the corolla.— This tenth Sefirah shows us Relativity realized in accordance with its essence, i.e., presenting the total system of constituent relationships: One-All, varied and complete. Thus *Yesod* and *Malkhuth* are in some way the splitting of the character of the Absolute contained in *Kether*: principle and end, center and periphery.

The figurative scheme of the Sefiroth system, in accordance with the regime of Balance, presents a direct connection of *Netsah* and *Hod* with *Malkhuth* (see figure V). Thus, *Malkhuth* communicates with these two Sefiroth immediately and mediately through *Yesod*. And this is understandable, given that Relativity is in fact made of a polarity linked by a relationship. It is the relationship that introduces unity into the polarity and permeates it with a function of the Absolute. *Malkhuth* and *Tifereth* both mark the identity of the Absolute and the Relative; but *Tifereth* makes Relativity shine in the radiance of the Absolute whereas *Malkhuth* fulfills the Absolute through the unfolding or blossoming of the Relative.

Through this whole process, *Da'ath* spreads. As we have seen, *Da'ath* is not a Sefirah,[7] but is the very fact of the union of the complementaries *Hokhmah* and *Binah*; and this fact is the immanent trace of the transcendent principle. Furthermore, *Da'ath* is represented by the cruciform arrangement of the Balance. It is the agent of all connections that sometimes emerge from *Kether* between *Hokhmah* and *Binah*, and sometimes link *Tifereth* to *Yesod*.

Da'ath, knowledge, knowing, is in short the principle of all relationships, the root of relationships plunging into the Absolute. But the polarity of the relationship necessarily has an origin distinct from the relationship

---

[7] Some diagrams position *Da'ath* between *Hokhmah* and *Binah* as a distinct Sefirah. This does not appear to be consistent with the teaching of the Zohar or the *Sefer Yetzirah*.—Some commentators say that *Da'ath* is manifested, while *Kether* remains hidden.

itself, because Relativity is due to the incomplete union of two polar terms. And in order for the union to be possible even while resisting the perfect identity that would transform Relativity into the Absolute, these polar terms must participate both in the character of the complementaries and in the character of the antagonists—they must correspond to the transition between these two characters. And it is to these transitive functions that *Netsah* and *Hod* would correspond.

III. The Hierarchy

We have just seen by what correlations the bilateral equilibrium of the Balance is established. It had necessarily to bring about the distribution of the Sefiroth into three ternaries, and the formation into three columns. We must now account for the number of these ternaries and find in the direction from top to bottom an equilibrium that keeps the extremes and intermediates in their place.

A superposition, or indefinite discontinuity, of ternaries would not satisfy the conditions of perfect equilibrium. It was just such a juxtaposition of the Sefiroth that had brought about the destruction of the first state of things. This stratification expressed the antinomy that results from the relationship between the Absolute and the Relative on account of the infinite distance separating them. Now, the purpose of the regime of the Balance is precisely to make the Absolute and the Relative, the upper and the lower, in some way interdependent, to reconcile the projection emanating from the Absolute with the aspiration of the Relative towards the Absolute, and to prevent the Relative from being repressed by the projection or absorbed by the aspiration. What is needed, then, is a regime that distributes these tendencies in such a way as to form an *organism*.

The two first ternaries are oriented in opposite directions, the second in some way reflecting the first. The meeting of these two ternaries enables the unfolding of two opposing tendencies: on the one hand, the complementaries *Hokhmah* and *Binah* bring identity to prevail over distinction; on the other, the antagonists *Hesed* and *Geburah* erase the identity behind the distinction. The complementaries arise through *analysis* of the principle; the antagonists achieve perfection through *synthesis*. Thus the upper senary from *Kether* to *Tifereth* appears as the manifestation of the Absolute in all its fullness.

This unfolding opens up every possibility to the Relative, but it doesn't determine its effectiveness; it projects universality, but it remains to establish individuality. From there, the transitive functions that, taken together, neutralize the two previous ternaries, in some way channel the manifestation and transform it into an operation, or *formation*. And this results in *Yesod*: the agent par excellence.

But here, the senary is replaced by a quaternary. Complementaries and antagonists, which are as it were the recto and verso of duality, have produced, along with principle and end, complete development. Here, the two faces of duality are replaced by the metamorphosis of one into the other: this constitutes transitivity realized as *operation*, represented by *Yesod*. Operation is, in fact, the transition between principle and end. It leads to the result.

But this result provides data drawn from the field of complete development. *Malkhuth* represents the adaptation of this development to the conditions of the Relative. *Malkhuth* is suspended vertically from *Yesod*. At the same time, two channels converge upon it, one coming from *Netsah*, the other from *Hod*, and this establishes a bilateral reaction to the operation planned by *Yesod*. The influence of the axis is thus transformed into a radiance that prevents it from being prolonged, and that avoids both confusion and rupture.

Let us now leave aside the vertical channels, which represent the relationships of hierarchy and subordination, and the horizontal channels, which mark the symmetries of the correlative terms, to consider only the oblique channels, which radiate and centralize (see figure VI).

We find first of all two quadrilaterals, one positioned above the other. The first is composed of *Kether*, *Hokhmah*, *Binah*, and *Tifereth*; the second, of *Tifereth*, *Netsah*, *Hod*, and *Malkhuth*. To get the other oblique channels, we will add a branch on each side. In the upper quaternary, these additional branches will diverge from *Tifereth* and be extended so as to terminate below the lateral vertices (*Binah* and *Hokhmah*) of the upper quadrilateral. This will give us *Geburah* and *Hesed*. In the lower quadrilateral, the branches will start out from the lateral vertices (*Hod* and *Netsah*) and converge below the lower vertex (*Yesod*) to form *Malkhuth*. This difference summarizes the contrast between the upper zone and the lower zone; and it is this that must explain why the series of superposed ternaries is exhausted.

This diagram strikes a balance between two opposing trends: divergence and convergence of the columns. Divergence represents the antagonism necessary for differentiation; convergence corresponds to the union of complementaries indispensable for the realization of the concrete. And no oblique channel connects *Hokhmah* to *Geburah* or *Binah* to *Hesed*. Thus, *Hesed* and *Geburah* mark the state of extreme opposition. In *Tifereth*, complementaries and antagonisms combine for perfection. From *Netsah* and *Hod* emerges the duality of agent and patient for efficacy.

The limitation of the process is thus established by the reversal of convergence and divergence. The divergence emanating from the center (*Tifereth*) is followed by the divergence emanating from the sides (from *Netsah* and *Hod*).—After the duality of the lateral terms (*Hokhmah* and *Hesed*, *Binah* and *Geburah*) comes the duality of the central column (*Yesod* and *Malkhuth*).—At the top, the duality on either side develops the conditions of Relativity (expansion–restriction); at the bottom, the duality extending along the axis characterizes the root of Relativity (action–passion). The first of these dualities is resolved in a synthesis (*Tifereth*); the second is compensated by the two lateral convergences of a transitive character (*Netsah* and *Hod*), which seem to constitute two currents of opposite direction between action and reaction.

There are only three distinct ternaries superposed, i.e., having no common term; but by virtue of the arrangement just described, six superposed ternaries can be recognized, two having their vertex at the top (*Kether–Hokhmah–Binah* and *Tifereth–Netsah–Hod*), four having their vertex at the bottom (*Hokhmah–Binah–Tifereth*, *Hesed–Geburah–Tifereth*, *Netsah–Hod–Yesod*, and *Netsah–Hod–Malkhuth*).

The first two ternaries subordinate the product (effect) to the cause; the other four tend towards an end. In *Tifereth* the end brings together at the same time a distinction of two degrees (*Hokhmah* and *Binah*; *Hesed* and *Geburah*) drawn from the principle (*Kether*). In *Yesod* and *Malkhuth*, finality is characterized by two degrees, corresponding to the *Netsah–Hod* duality that *Tifereth* projected. Thus, in both cases, the tendency towards the end manifests a double current, while the projection of the principle is simple. This is interesting to ponder.

The relationships established by the oblique channels highlight a set of compensations that allows the assimilation between the incommensurable terms of the Absolute and the Relative. The influx that goes from *Kether* to *Malkhuth* thus propagates with the alternation of a lateral expansion and contraction that changes the all-powerful projection and aspiration of the Absolute into a vital rhythm. The aim of the hierarchy of the Balance is not to assert the supremacy of the Absolute over the Relative, but to acclimate the Relative to the intimate penetration of the Absolute.

Finally, let us observe that the system's hierarchy has the task of making the principle and its result, the means and the end, mutually supportive. If we speak of lower and higher, it is because this solidarity is the condition of the *creation, formation*, and *action* that constitute Relativity. But this process seen in God, as his *emanation*, does not constitute a degradation from higher to lower, but a transformation of aspect. The Zohar tells us that *Malkhuth* designates the Holy Spirit, from which it follows (as de Pauly notes) that this tenth Sefirah alone is just as important as the other nine combined, because the Holy Spirit is part of the very essence of God. *Malkhuth* is therefore God in his entirety as *Kether*. But *Kether* is God inaccessible to Relativity. *Malkhuth*, then, is God drawing from himself the development of all Relativity.

To the hierarchy of Sefiroth correspond the three or four worlds. The entire Sefiroth system constitutes the world of *emanation* (Atziluth), that is to say the system of conditions that bring together the Absolute and the Relative. It is the norm of all making and all subsistence. And this norm will be found in any reality that attains to being-in-itself, i.e., that fulfills a function of the Absolute. Without this function, a thing exists only as an accident, or a phenomenon—or, which amounts to the same thing, it only exists with regard to something else. And the complete set of Relative existences will have to reproduce the Sefiroth system.

After *emanation,* which establishes the conditions for the possibility of the Relative, comes the world of *creation* (Briah or Beriah), the passage from non-being to being, followed by the world of *formation* (Yetzirah), or the development of the intelligible conditions without which nothing can subsist. Briah, it seems, is the world of "substances" or noumena—i.e., of beings-in-themselves, beings that play the role of absolutes in connection to certain relations. Isaac Luria tells us that Briah is the world of souls. He thus seems to admit that the only possible substances are souls; and in our view, when critically examined, the concept of substance results in it being regarded as an immaterial entity. Yetzirah would then be the world of forces and laws, i.e., the world of the principles that direct actions. The ancients saw these principles in the sidereal world, which they considered immutable. And finally there is the world of *action* (Assiah), the world of facts or phenomena that concern the pure efficacy of that which is subject to becoming.

The last three worlds are placed hierarchically below the world of Atziluth. The ten Sefiroth of Atziluth (or emanation) provide these three worlds with a framework, and on this framework each world is further modeled into a system of Sefiroth. This leads to many correspondences, upon which, however, we cannot here dwell. But we do need find in the Atziluth system the conditions of this hierarchy of the four worlds itself. Now, from what has been said above, we can readily understand that the higher ternary (*Kether–Hokhmah–Binah*) corresponds to *emanation*. This ternary marks, in fact, the constitution of the divine essence itself, and the intimate union of these three Sefiroth with each other and with the *En-Sof*.

The second ternary (*Hesed–Geburah–Tifereth*) corresponds to *creation*. Indeed, *Hesed* is the gift, the magnificence; *Geburah* is separation, rigorous distribution; *Tifereth* is the synthesis, the perfect construction, and the external manifestation.

The third ternary (*Netsah–Hod–Yesod*) corresponds to *formation*,[8] that is, to work carried out by intelligences and applied to given data. Victory, honor, and foundation clearly mark the fecundity of this operation.

Finally, *Malkhuth* corresponds to the world of *action,* understanding "action" here not as *making things* but as *establishing relationships* (as opposed to making laws). And that is where Relativity comes in.

---

[8] Formation as education or training, as "forming the mind." ED

These four worlds correspond with the human organism. To emanation corresponds the head (thought, conception); to creation correspond the arms and the heart (desire, signs, dispositions); to formation correspond the thighs and genitals (generation, movement). Finally, action (or rather, phenomenon) lies underfoot; it receives the seeds and traces of movement and constitutes the support of Relativity, which maintains its existence solely by becoming-through-action.

IV. Concept of the Sexes

We have just seen in the Balance of the Sefiroth system the equilibrium established between the opposing terms of a duality through a central column; and then a second equilibrium between action and reaction, between the higher and the lower. This second equilibrium does not entail immobility, but a perpetual and living exchange of relationships that maintains a cohesive and conservative order. The bilateral equilibrium, then, must also allow movement.

The Balance is not an apparatus brought into equilibrium once and for all by means of fixed and equal loads on both sides. It is intended to weigh variable loads. Either of its two scales can tilt. It thus serves to establish, by comparison, which of two bodies is the heavier. But in truth, this capacity for comparison is its least significant property. The mission of the Balance is above all to relate the weights of all bodies to a standard, to establish a classification of all objects under the notion of weight. Moreover, this notion of weight is very closely connected in turn to the notion of existence, because it expresses existence through the possibility of action. Through this function, the Balance symbolizes the *highest function of thought* with regard to all things Relative—which is to unify, synthesize, and classify diversity according to the absolute scale of values.

Although the two scales of a balance respond in the same way to weights placed on them, they do not both play the same role in the weighing: in one scale we place an object of unknown weight, in the other a standard weight. Thus, the bilateral equilibrium of the Balance realizes a double relationship: one of *coordination* (in a sense real), establishes the equilibrium and maintains it; and one of *subordination* (in a sense ideal), which evaluates a variable object by a fixed standard. The first relationship concerns the state of real things, the second refers to goals.

Now, the configuration of the Sefiroth system according to the Balance has just this double character. The linear series is not overridden by the distribution into three columns and superposed ternaries. The left remains subordinate to the right. Also, the right always represents more union, the left more distinction or differentiation. So, although the terms of the right and left columns are located on the same level as opposite poles, these poles are differentiated, such that a current flows from one to the other in a defined direction.

Through the operation of weighing, the polarity of the Balance is differentiated, just like the polarity of electromagnetism differentiates positive and negative charge, just like right and left (which are asymmetric in human beings both from a mechanical and from a fluidic point of view) are differentiated. And finally, through this differentiation in function between the two sides, the Balance represents the great principle of sexuality. The male (right) side is higher and tends towards synthesis; the female (left) side is lower and tends towards analysis. And so the principle of separation and the principle of union form the supreme combination, preserving the radical separation that leads to nothingness, and the confusion that leads to pantheism. We will not insist further on this point because, owing to its importance, it would lead us beyond the framework we have imposed on ourselves in this study. Let us just note that, thanks to the difference between the two sides, the bilateral equilibrium and the sustaining (upright) equilibrium avoid immobility and crystallization, which would be the negation of life. The two equilibriums combine; they allow a current to oscillate from one side to the other, giving rise to an ascending or descending wave, depending on whether we consider the creature's elevation towards God or God's abasement towards the creature.

This differentiation of right and left corresponds to the

relationship between male and female. According to the
Zohar, it is "in some way like male and female." Now, the
relationship between male and female does not exactly
correspond to that of activity and passivity: the female is
receptive, but not passive; the male is primarily a doer or
leader, not simply active. The operation is common to
both male and female, but they oppose each other as
action and reaction—and this contains both a correlation
and a subordination relationship. Reaction presupposes
action, but action only comes about through reaction:
agent and reactant are thus given correlatively as conditions of the result. But the passage from conditions to
effect is determined by the male; the female[9] can do
nothing before the male intervenes. So there is a combination of equilibrium and current.

The Zohar presents the modality of the sexes in the divine
as intimately linked to the Balance. But in describing the
restitution that followed the breaking of the vessels, the
Kabbalah of the commentators has the sexes pass through
various phases of reconciliation, the meaning of which we
will not here investigate. Let us just note that the *face-to-
face* stance seems to signify pure, self-conscious thought;
the *back-to-back* stance would then signify the antithesis
of spiritual and material limiting and not knowing each
other; and the *face-to-back* stance would signify either

---

[9] At least among humans and other mammals.

thought seeking to dominate matter or matter aspiring to assimilate mind. The breaking of the vessels was brought on by the antagonism of the characters of the Absolute and the Relative: identity and distinction. Through the interplay of the sexes, the Balance will harmoniously combine these two characters. It will establish the face-to-face—the penetration of all things by thought—by means of the two degrees of intimacy derived from the principle of sexuality marking, respectively, predominance of identity and distinction. That is, the constant, inherent coupling[10] of nature characterizes the intimate, essential union constituting the reality of the Absolute (it corresponds more directly to thought), and coupling alternating with separation characterizes the predominance of Relativity, in which duality prevails over unity (it corresponds to life). But the influence of the Absolute must be found within the Relative itself. Duality cannot prevail without being ordered, and it therefore tends to transform correlation into subordination, whereas within the Absolute, duality is maintained by evoking this subordination, but then remains more effaced.

The Balance therefore distributes the two sexes according to their normal order. It corresponds to the essential condition of man created male and female and in whom the female is then taken from the male. The first of these two stages seems to correspond to the union of the father

---

[10] French *copulation*: coupling in the sense of *coniunctio*. ED

and mother and the second to the union of the king and queen. At the top, *Hokhmah* and *Binah* represent the father and mother, whose coupling is *constant*: since the creation of the Balance they have always been face-to-face. One could say that *Da'ath* is their very coupling. It is so intimate and so immediate that here correlation obliterates the direction of the current, which is remembered only by the ranks of *Hokhmah* and *Binah* in linear order. Their begotten, *Tifereth* or the king, signifies the synthesis of the two sexes, with predominance to the male principle. Between the king (*Tifereth*) and queen (*Malkhuth*), coupling *alternates* with separation, and the face-to-face with back-to-back—that, the direction of the current predominates over the correlation that occurs in the union. And here the mediating term is not, like *Da'ath*, the very fact of coupling, but a distinct Sefirah, *Yesod*, which represents the mediating organ of the covenant (*alliance*). Thus, where coupling is inherent to the very nature of the spouses, the correlation of the sexes dominates; where the sexes remain separate and are brought together by action, the current from male to female becomes predominant.

V. Notion of Persons

It is to the notion of persons to which the notion of male and female is most directly attached. The long-suffering (prior to the sexual distinction) occupies *Kether*; the father has *Hokhmah* as his seat; the mother, *Binah*; the king, *Tifereth*; and the queen, *Malkhuth*. But this order is merely an adaptation of the order of persons to the order of Sefiroth.[11]

This is not the only influence of the notion of persons and degrees of sexuality in the Balance system. The three degrees of union between the sexes overlap in depth. The long-suffering penetrates the Sefiroth from top to bottom; it is clothed up to the level of *Hokhmah* and *Binah* by the father and mother. The king and queen cover the father and mother in the region below *Hesed* and *Geburah*.

This deep penetration marks the grading of the relationship between the Absolute and the Relative by a more

---

[11] "The chief *Partsufim* [persons] are five in number. Where the flowing potencies of pure mercy and divine love which are contained in the supreme Sefirah are gathered together in a personal figure, there, according to the Zohar, arises the configuration of *Arikh Anpin*, sometimes translated 'The Long Face,' but actually signifying 'the Long-Suffering,' i.e., God the long-suffering and merciful. In the Zohar, *Arikh Anpin* is also called *Attika Kaddisha*, that is, 'the Holy Ancient One.' The potencies of the Sefiroth of divine wisdom and intelligence, *Hokhmah* and *Binah*, have become the *Partsufim* of 'Father and Mother,' *Abba* and *Imma*. The potencies of the six lower Sefiroth (with the exception of the *Shekhinah*), in which therefore mercy, justice, and compassion are in harmonious balance, are organized into a single configuration, *Zeir Anpin*. Again, the correct translation is not 'The Short Face,' but 'The Impatient,' as opposed to 'The Long-Suffering.' In this configuration, the quality of stern judgment, which has no place in the figure of the 'Holy Ancient One,' plays an important part." Scholem, *Major Trends*.

intimate mode than the previous ones. The order of up and down, right and left, and their combining through a current, explicitly revealed the ternary that constitutes reality in terms of thought: it distinguished polarity and transcendence, then linked them together. Here, the relationship between the Absolute and the Relative is shown to be a penetration that is somehow organic, vital, fundamentally unifying. The Absolute shows itself through the Relative as its framework, with the Relative as its covering or envelope. This is the most intimate evocation of man's bodily constitution: *bone* and *flesh*. Woman is indeed "bone of his bone and flesh of his flesh," since the notion of the sexes is represented at the three levels of depth.

This last relationship opens up new metaphysical horizons. In all the above, we have assumed a connection between the Absolute and the Relative: the entire theory of the Sefiroth is based on this idea. And yet the antinomy of the Relative and the Absolute still stands before us. Between the Absolute and the Relative no relation seems possible, because compared to the Absolute the Relative is nothing. Every relationship presupposes two terms, and here one of the terms vanishes in front of the other. This did not escape St Thomas Aquinas. He conceived this relationship as in some way unilateral, as having reality only on the side of the Relative. The creature refers to God, but God cannot be the subject of any real relation of which the creature would be the term. So, in order to avoid the contradictory aspects of the idea of relation, we have spoken, not of a relation, but of a connection (*rapport*), between the Absolute and the Relative, i.e., of the "virtuality" of the relation.

But the multi-degree envelopment of the persons by which the Sefiroth system is vivified, together with the story of the restitution of the vessels, give us a glimpse of the sublime solution that makes possible a relationship between the Relative and the Absolute.

Being nothing in itself, the capacity of the Relative to react in some way to the Absolute is null. And the breaking of the vessels seems to point to impotence as the only possible manifestation of the Relative when left to its own devices. It is then that the Absolute comes to project itself, as it were, to the depths of Relativity, to adopt its nature, to incarnate itself therein in order to communicate to it the faculty of reacting to the Absolute while nevertheless remaining Relative. And that, it seems, is what this deep penetration symbolizes: the perfecting of the Sefiroth system. From absolute Thought flowed the conditions of Relativity; then absolute Life came and lay its germ of absoluteness deep within Relativity, and assimilates the influx emitted by thought. And so, under the rays of the supreme sun, the system of Relativity has risen as the Tree of Life, identifying itself with the Man-God and representing as an organism the synthesis of the essential faculties expressed by the Sefiroth.

Finally, we have four concomitant notions in the Sefiroth system: (1) The linear sequence indicates the order that follows from the subordination of the Relative to the Absolute; it calls for hierarchy. (2) The equilibrium of the Balance arises from the duality implied in Relativity, establishing it through correlation, and bringing about equilibrium. (3) The notion of sexes is introduced by differentiation, which brings about the combination of subordination and correlation; it gives rise to current and oscillation. (4) And finally, the hierarchy of persons is brought about by the transcendence of the Absolute; it achieves its immanence in the Relative.

And so the antinomy of the Relative and the Absolute is resolved by the conjunction of thought and life. Through the Sefiroth, the Absolute establishes the conditions of Relativity; through the persons, Relativity is actualized in the likeness of the Absolute.[12]

---

[12] Par les Sefiroth l'Absolu fonde les conditions de la Relativité, par les Personnes la Relativité se trouve actualisée à l'instar de l'Absolu.

Deductions and Correspondences of the Sefiroth

I. The Sefiroth and Numbers

THE BALANCE system includes ten Sefiroth connected by twenty-two channels that correspond to the twenty-two Hebrew letters. If therefore the limitation of the number of Sefiroth and the distribution of channels is sufficiently justified, we will have the key to the doctrine that reduces the entire composition of the universe to ten numbers and twenty-two letters. It is in the system of Sefiroth constructed according to the Balance that the principle of the decad of the esoteric doctrines, and of the Pythagoreans, is probably to be found. Other considerations, notably that drawn from the sum $1 + 2 + 3 + 4 = 10$, are, in our opinion, only derivative. It is because the Balance metaphysically implies unity, duality, ternary, and quaternary, that this sum of the first four numbers (i.e., the denary) expresses integral fulfillment. Unity, duality, and ternary are evident here: quaternary is less striking.

But, since we still find quinary, senary, septenary, octenary, and novenary, it is necessary to show that these latter numerical principles are only derivative, whereas the quaternary is primitive.

The quaternary is primitive because the ternary alone would not give rise to any development. The ternary is only concrete by bringing out a double role in the unity dominating the duality—i.e., this unity must be principle and result at the same time. The quaternary is thus implicated virtually in the ternary. It is by distinguishing the two functions of principle and result that the quaternary is realized. The middle column in the Sefiroth system represents the introduction of the quaternary. It is therefore essential.

What is more, the three ternaries require a tenth term to bring them together: *Malkhuth*. This further manifests the quaternary and relegates the novenary to a secondary status.

Sometimes we say there are nine Sefiroth, but it is always with the implication that the tenth is the container (*Kether*) or the resultant (*Malkhuth*). In fact, the triple ternary is a completion only on condition that it achieves a unity like the primitive ternary—and just as the ternary at the same time posits the quaternary, so the novenary brings the denary, without which metaphysical unity is not achieved. The quaternary results from the junction that takes place within the middle term, between the identity and distinction of the two opposites. It is the relationship of the element to the whole that brings about the denary.

Hd ——————— K

M

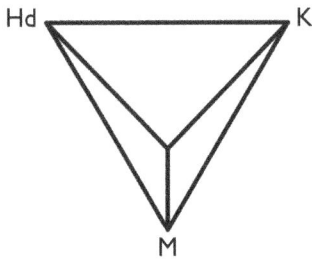

In the Balance, the ternary is represented by the superposition of three groups of three, or by the juxtaposition of three columns. This double construction gives the novenary. The middle column provides tenth term.

The novenary by 5 + 4 is very important; it seems to express the opposition of individuality and universality, both taken in concrete form. We would form it in the Balance by disregarding either *Kether* or *Malkhuth* and attaching *Tifereth* to either the upper or lower quaternary. If we take the ten Sefiroth and link *Tifereth* to the lower half, of which it is the starting-point, we obtain the denary by 5 + 5. It contrasts the universal expansion of the Absolute with its concentration in individual form, the womb with the embryo it contains.

The quaternary is represented first of all by two axial quadrilaterals, *Kether–Hokhmah–Binah–Tifereth* (figure III) and *Tifereth–Netsah–Hod–Yesod* (figure IV),[1] which we examined before. This is its primary manifestation, due to the interweaving of the principle of act (origin–result) and the principle of polarity (thought–reality).

Secondly, it constructs the rectangle *Hokhmah–Binah–*

---

[1] This last quaternary seems to correspond to the four animals of the chariot of Ezekiel.

Hesed–Geburah, which leads from the complementaries to the antagonists, and the rectangle *Hesed–Geburah–Netsah–Hod*, which reduces the antagonists to transitives. These are derived quaternaries; they consist in establishing two degrees in the opposition that constitutes one of the two principles (principle of act or principle of polarity): it does this by applying in turn the union and distinction resulting from both of the two principles. Finally, the quaternary manifests itself yet again in an intensive form in the triangle formed by *Netsah–Hod–Malkhuth* and having *Yesod* as center. It seems to express the relationship of the agent (*Yesod*) and the patient (*Malkhuth*) with dynamic (*Netsah*) and static (*Hod*) circumstances, which latter influence both agent and patient and are directly related to each other.

The senary, as we have seen, represents plenitude through the first six Sefiroth, which lead to *Tifereth*. There remains a quaternary of adaptation. The whole gives the denary by 6 + 4. The primitive senary, which goes from *Kether* to *Tifereth*, transforms into a group of five Sefiroth, *Hesed–Geburah–Netsah–Hod–Yesod*, that surrounds *Tifereth*. This set is called the little face (*Zeir Anpin*). It is the king. It indicates in some way the divine man who is espoused to the universe (figured by *Malkhuth*) and who proceeds from the father and the mother. If we disregard its fecundity in *Yesod*, what remains is a quinary formed by the four extremities and a center. This characterizes man as an absolute personality, operating the synthesis of the derived quaternary—that is to say of the double polarity of antagonisms and transitions.

If we combine *Malkhuth* with the six other lower Sefiroth, we obtain the septenary. It is only in this form that it appears in the Balance. It is formed by the union of the king (senary) with the queen: a final, enveloping, unity. The septenary is therefore not represented here by 3 + 4 or by 5 + 2, but by 6 + 1: like Sabbath. The Sabbath is the lower reflection of the Jubilee (7 x 7) located in *Binah*—the mother above, whose access is by the fiftieth gate (7^2 + 1) of intelligence. The union of the three upper Sefiroth constitutes the denary by 3 + 7.

The septenary by 3 + 4 establishes the union of the tendency towards the concrete absolute (3) and towards concrete relativity (4), developed by the derived quaternary mentioned above. We would find the 3 + 4 septenary by comparing the number of terms in each side column to the number of terms in the middle column. But this point of view seems uninteresting to us.

The septenary by 5 + 2 seems even more secondary: it pits concrete individuality (5) against an opposition (2). By 5 + 2, we could oppose to the *Yesod–Malkhuth* duality the quinary formed by *Tifereth* and the four Sefiroth that surround it. This would summarize the opposition between the absolute resolution of antinomies accomplished in *Tifereth* and the regime of action and reaction that brings about the relative resolution of antinomies.

The octenary has no significant representation in the Sefiroth system. It draws its main value from the opposition of two quaternaries, and as such corresponds to the principle of action and reaction. This is the energy cycle. Like 7 + 1, the octenary is the initial term of a new world. The forms 5 + 3 and 2 + 6 seem wholly secondary.

We have already spoken about the important formations of the denary.

As for the duodenary, it, like the octenary, is derived by 3 x 4 or 2 x 6, and as such, it is the evolution cycle. It therefore corresponds to a point of view of periodicity that remains foreign to the conception of the Sefiroth. It would be necessary to examine the form 5 + 7, which seems to express the alliance of concrete individuality and the universal reciprocity of principles and their developments. But this relationship also remains foreign to the Sefiroth system.

The number thirteen seems intimately linked to the faces, and thereby indirectly to the Sefiroth. It is the number of the tufts of the beard and of the ways of mercy; but it would involve us in a study we cannot undertake here.

Finally, let us point out that the meeting of the ten numbers and the twenty-two letters corresponds to the

[2] The Idra Rabba represents the supreme wisdom through the brain, and the thirty-two paths that spread throughout the body the influx of wisdom. Anatomy in fact lists thirty-two perforations at the base of the

thirty-two ways or paths of wisdom.[2] And indeed, if the Balance system is the ingenious invention of the wisdom who conceived the creation, conservation, and evolution of the Relative, the constitutive elements of this system rightly bear the name of the ways or paths of wisdom.

As for the fifty gates of intelligence, they indicate the influence of *Binah*—that sort of matrix where all that emanates from God is elaborated.

Sometimes these Sefiroth are distributed 7 x 7, to each of the seven lower Sefiroth: that makes forty-nine. *Binah* is then the fiftieth gate. This seems to express that each lower Sefirah must reflect within itself the seven others.

Sometimes, the fifty gates are distributed 10 x 10 to the five Sefiroth that follow *Binah*, i.e., *Tifereth* and the four Sefiroth that surround it. This seems to express the centralization of all emanation around *Tifereth* through the mediation of *Binah*. Each of these five Sefiroth then reflects the entire system.

This distribution is symbolized by the five leaves of salvation that surround the rose (*Malkhuth*).

The 7 x 7 distribution indicates the progression and adaptation of the higher towards *Binah*, the mediatrix between creatures and the supreme Trinity. The distribu-

---

skull through which nerves and vessels pass. In the *Book of the Royal Valley*, the thirty-two paths are compared to the thirty-two teeth and their interstices, which form an enclosure for the organs of the Word and which, on the other hand, emoliate the objects coming from outside to render them suitable for integration into life.

tion by ten signals the perfection of the system in the fullness of manifestation, a fullness brought about by the mediation of *Binah*.

Finally, there are seventy-two branches issued by *Hesed* and *Geburah*. This number is that of the most developed divine name, the genesis of which we examine in our study *The Divine Names*.

II. The Sefiroth and the Constitution of Man

The Sefiroth system based on the Balance also retraces the organic schema of man.

The first ternary (*Kether–Hokhmah–Binah*) is the head. Sometimes the three supreme Sefiroth and *Da'ath* are considered as three or four brains (probably the two cerebral hemispheres, the cerebellum, and the spinal cord), affirming the intimate union of the components of thought. In other accounts, *Kether* represents the skull, *Hokhmah* the brain, *Binah* the throat or tongue.

Hesed and *Geburah* correspond to the arms; and one would be tempted to lower the right arm or open the right hand and raise the left arm or close the left hand.

Tifereth is the heart, focus of individuality. The ternary *Hesed–Geburah–Tifereth* expresses centralization around the subject.

Netsah and *Hod* are assimilated to the legs; and we would see the right leg put forward, the left leg supporting.[3] *Yesod* marks the organ of generation. This ternary *Netsah–Hod–Yesod* represents the movement of the subject outside itself. Finally, *Malkhuth* is under the feet, serving as support.

The five degrees of the soul correspond to the five persons of Kabbalah: the ancient of days or long-suffering; the father and the mother; the king and the queen. These degrees, like these persons, indicate, through their conditions of sexuality, the phases that link the intimate identification of the components of absolute reality to their separation. The hierarchy of persons marks the more or less intimate union of relative life with absolute life. The degrees of the soul present the same phases in the relationship of relative thought with absolute thought.

The Sefiroth correspond to both the persons and to the degrees of the soul. In general, the long-suffering is associated with *Kether*, the father with *Hokhmah*, the mother with *Binah*, the king with *tifereth*, the queen with *Malkhuth*. As regards the soul: *Yechidah* (unitive soul) corresponds to the long-suffering; *Chaiah* (vital soul) to the father; *Neschamah* (intellectual soul, *mens*) to the mother; *Ruach* (psychic soul) to the king; *Nephesh* (vegetative soul) to the mother. But I must limit myself to

---

[3] The attitude we have just described is that of the beautiful Greek statue in the Louvre that was first called Mars, then Achilles. This statue also tilts its head to the right.

these summary indications, because the study of the persons and the degrees of the soul exceeds the bounds of this study. I point out, however, that the correspondence established between the Sefiroth on one hand, and the persons and the degrees of the soul on the other, is not absolutely fixed.

The same can be said of the correspondence of the Sefiroth with the four letters of the tetragrammaton. From a certain point of view, the Yod is applied to *Kether*, the first Hé to *Hokhmah*, the Waw to *Binah*, and the second Hé to *Malkhuth*. At the same time, the three supreme Sefiroth correspond to the three persons of the Holy Trinity, and *Malkhuth* to the community of Israel or to the Church. Other times, the Yod is assigned to both *Kether* and *Hokhmah*, the Hé to *Binah*, the Waw to *Tifereth*, and the second Hé to *Malkhuth*. Let us content ourselves with pointing out these correspondences: it is not possible to examine them in detail here.

III. Systems Related to the Sefiroth

Our mind cannot embrace the hyper-concrete nature of metaphysical realities in a single view. To grasp it, the mind varies its points of view. And these points of view themselves refer to each other by virtue of their common object. Hence the analogical correspondences.

However, the Sefiroth system seeks to express the conditions of all creation, all conservation, and all progress.

So any set of realities constituted as a system (i.e., acquiring autonomy under the regime of relationship) cannot be formed, conserved, or perfected without imitating the system of the Sefiroth and presenting an image of it.

According to this principle, the Kabbalists attempted to establish the Sefirotic pattern in various groupings. We will limit ourselves to listing a few of these applications, because we lack the data to verify their value.

In Knorr we find the Sefiroth of light, distributed in a circle; the Sefiroth constituting the parts of the head of the long face: those applied to *Hokhmah* taken as the upper part of the face, and those applied to *Binah* taken as the lower part of the face (region of the mouth). The Sefiroth correspond to the whole body.

Note as well that the Sefiroth can be applied to the worlds of angels, to the stars, to metals, to the petitions of the Lord's Prayer, to celestial palaces, to the empire of the demon, etc.

The principle that leads commentators to look everywhere for analogies with the Sefiroth is perfectly rational, since this system seems to be the canon of all possible systematization. But we must be careful not to draw hasty and superficial analogies. We need to be certain that the ten terms which seem to be grouped together are indeed essential functions, and therefore meet the necessary and sufficient conditions for a genuine system. Now, in order to make this demonstration, it was necessary to determine by what intelligible relationships the Sefiroth relate to each other. In our opinion, the "Law of Creation of all Reality" brought to light by Wronski makes it possible to discern, among the countless analogies, those that in all likelihood are based on the very essence of things. This Law of Creation appears to us to be the explanation (if not complete, at least already very advanced) of the system of the Balance. It has been our constant guide during this work.

If, in accordance with the above, Wronski's Law of Creation is the discursive and analytical exposition of the Balance system, it was nonetheless established by pure reasoning, and so its concordance with the Balance system would tend to prove that this system corresponds to a metaphysical necessity. And this is all the less surprising given that, throughout all the esoteric doctrines of antiquity, we find conceptions that are more or less closely akin to the Sefiroth system.

If these doctrines have independent origins, this remarkable convergence of esoteric conceptions tends to indicate that this decad necessarily imposes itself on human thought as soon as it turns towards the Absolute. If this relationship comes from an identity of source, the fact that this doctrine has been universally accepted shows that it provides the most satisfactory solution to the problem of the Absolute. It would therefore be very interesting to follow the trace of the Sefirotic conception through the sacred books, monuments, and legends of antiquity. But we may well wonder whether current archaeological knowledge is extensive enough for this research to prove fruitful.

So, without focusing on the examination of the Egyptian Ennead, the Amshaspands of the *Avesta*, an ancient Tai Chi chart, etc., we will limit ourselves to mentioning a few conceptions closely resembling the Sefiroth system.

Let us first mention the system expounded in *L'Initiation* (by Marc Haven, after Pictet) and attributed to a Druidic tradition:

LOVE

WISDOM   FORCE

GOOD   JUSTICE

BEAUTY

DECLINE   GROWTH

GENERATION

ABRED
(WORLD)

Above is *Ceugant*, analogue of *En-Sof*.
Below is *Annwn*, the abyss.

This Druidic system seems to proceed quite directly from that of Kabbalah. Here, the concrete, total unity of the crown is translated by what is its very realization, i.e., by love. Here, force replaces *Binah*. It is opposed to the choice represented by wisdom, as the faculty of producing everything; yet, the first principle of all power or force is knowledge: the supreme force is therefore identified with intelligence. And it is easy to see how growth corresponds to *Netsah*. But it is difficult to understand decline as an analogue of *Hod*.

The layout of the whole, however, corresponds exactly to that of the Sefirotic Balance.

Monterregio, in his *Mathesis*,[4] points out a decad, attributed to the Hindus, that presents quite remarkable analogies with the Sefiroth, although also deviating from it in a significant way. In any case, the general point of view is not the same, as described below.

The system of the Sefiroth seeks to deduce from the conception of the Absolute the possibility of the Relative; it shows the Relative as subordinate to the Absolute, as extracted from its fullness. Here, the emanation of the Absolute is seen as a condition of creation.

The Hindu system outlined in *Mathesis*, on the other hand, seems to consider the construction of the Relative. Principle and Absolute figure here as virtuality, while Reality and Perfection are achieved in the fullness of the Relative. We have seen that *Kether* and *Malkhuth* are not

---

[4] Jean Malfati de Monterregio, *La Mathèse ou anarchie et hiérarchie de la Science* [Mathesis, or anarchy and hierarchy in science] (repr. 1946).

opposed as the higher and the lower, but as the ipseity (selfhood) and alterity (otherness) of God. God's self-hood calls for the notion of the Absolute; his otherness is conceived as the fullness of the Relative—the Trinity from which emerges the quaternary of the tetragrammaton.

The Hindu system in Monterregio's *Mathesis* presents the passage from the generating Principle to the result as a construction of the concrete by means of the abstract. The Kabbalah system deduces the result from the fullness of the source; here, the generating principle seems transcendent to its origin. The result of this difference in viewpoints is that the entities that make up the Hindu system are subordinate to numbers and geometric figures. The Sefiroth system, on the other hand, has dominion over the characters of numbers and contains their principles. Finally, in Monterregio's presentation we see nothing recalling the notion of the Balance. To us, this system appears to constitute a derivative of the Sefiroth system as applied to cosmology and psychology. And that gives it remarkable interest.

Oswald Wirth pointed out a correspondence between the Sefiroth and the first ten Major Arcana of the Tarot. The Magician, source of all activity and thought, would correspond to *Kether*; the High Priestess or Isis to *Hokhmah*; the Empress to *Binah*; the Emperor (magnificence) to *Hesed*; the Pope (duty, moral law) to *Geburah*; the Lovers (beauty, heart) to *Tifereth*; the Chariot (coordinating and directing principle) to *Netsah*; Justice (immutable law, order of nature) to *Hod*; the Hermit (condensed energy) to *Yesod*; the Wheel of Fortune (cycle, phenomenal totality) to *Malkhuth*. Here is material for an in-depth study that we cannot here undertake.

A word, finally, on the analogies one would be tempted to seek between the Sefiroth and the conceptions of Baselides and Valentinus. The gnostic school seems to have focused especially on the problem Kabbalah leaves in the shadows: the fall of the vessels. The ogdoad, the decad, and the dodecad of Valentinus are designed, it seems, with a view to explaining the fall and its restitution. If this is so, it is with the anterior and the transitive state of the Sefiroth and not with the system of the Balance that they should be contrasted.

More recently, Jacob Boehme's septenary, and in this century Wronski's Law of Creation, are closely linked to the Sefiroth system: but these relationships will require special studies.

IV. Metaphysical Anthropomorphism

The Sefiroth system built on the model of man and the layout of the Balance, which establishes the cycle of numbers and letters and is based on the ideas of sexuality and personhood is, in our opinion, the most concrete metaphysical conception the human brain has produced. It condenses into a single body the essential orders through which our thought moves: mathematical and logical abstraction, aesthetic figuration, dynamic representation, psychic appetite.

The nature of man constitutes the mediating essence between the Absolute and the Relative: this is the idea on which the objective value of all Kabbalah rests and that justifies its claim to express absolute Reality through symbols. It is through this idea alone, in fact, that metaphysics can escape Kant's *Critique*, according to which all speculations regarding the transcendent domain are only benchmarks for our use, intended to lend order to the domain of immanence.

We can in fact only know something about transcendent reality if our nature is in relationship with the Absolute. And the faculty that fulfills this role is reason.

But Kant restricted the transcendent scope of reason to the idea of duty. And yet, if the law of duty is not justified by any speculative notion having the character of the Absolute, Kant's categorical imperative is nothing more than a fascination lacking legitimate authority, a more or less advantageous rule to guide us.

If we admit, on the contrary, that the principles of speculative reason have an absolute foundation, we are led to the transcendent anthropomorphism of the Zohar: i.e., human thought can derive from its own principles an image resembling metaphysical reality.

Now, we can establish that the principles of our thought have an absolute value. The notion of reality vanishes if reality does not relate to any thought; and every thought implies a relationship between two terms. This fundamental condition of thought introduces within the very heart of reality the relationship that arises first of all with the character of the Absolute. And thought in turn, because of the relationship of which it is the principle and which is the absolute foundation of all relationships, asserts itself as something real and absolute.

It is therefore impossible to deny these principles an absolute value without undermining the distinction between the Relative and the Absolute. Man therefore recognizes that the essence of his own thinking (and consequently of the very essence of his nature) consists in mediating between the Relative and the Absolute. It follows from this that anthropomorphism is not simply a representation of metaphysical reality, distorted for our particular use, but that it expresses the very nature of this reality, albeit through veils that can distort it. This is the principle implicit in the Kabbalah.

But when we say that metaphysical reality is constituted as a man, it is of course a question of man considered in his essence and not in his special form of rational vertebrate, a form that results from the adaptation of the human essence in our era and our planet.

The essence of man is to be a *rational animate being*. In

him takes place the alliance between the Absolute, which is the object of reason, and the fullness of autonomous relation, which is life. Reason is the Absolute as the source of relationship; life is the medium through which pure relativity (which in itself reduces to nothingness) acquires a being of its own.

Thus conceived, the essence of man appears as a principle derived immediately from the Absolute to establish reason and life, these two functions of the Absolute making themselves immanent to the Relative to enable it to subsist and to manifest itself in it. In its capacity as mediator, human nature participates in both the Absolute and the Relative. We must therefore find within it the Absolute adapting to the Relative and the Relative adapting to the Absolute.

The Absolute is united with the Relative by human nature, making Himself a creature, without His essence as Creator and Absolute ceasing to be incommunicable. And this constitutes the God-man. The Relative assimilates the Absolute through the seeds of absoluteness that God sows within it. And these children of God are purely human creatures. Finally, the result of mediation must be to unite in a single body the God-made-man and the human beings called to share in divine life.

This is the central idea that underpins the entire Kabbalah and gives its metaphysical anthropomorphism an objective value.

This metaphysical anthropomorphism was definitively

formulated among the commentators of the Zohar by the notion of Adam Kadmon. It seems very clear that this notion is nothing other than the metaphysical explanation of the dogma of the Incarnation of the Word in the person of Christ or the Messiah.

Christianity presents the Incarnation of the second person of the Holy Trinity as an historical fact accomplished in the form of an individual of our human and earthly species in the person of Jesus Christ. The concept of Adam Kadmon, without specifying when and in what special form the Incarnation of the Word takes place, considers God-made-man to be implied by Creation itself.[5]

We would not dare say that these two conceptions necessarily entail each other, but it seems that, far from contradicting each other, they complete each other.

---

[5] "This brings us to a further aspect of the doctrine of the *Tikkun*. The process in which God conceives, brings forth, and develops himself does not reach its final conclusion in God. Certain parts of the process of restitution are allotted to Man. Not all the lights which are held in captivity by the powers of darkness are set free by their own efforts; it is Man who adds the final touch to the divine countenance; it is he who completes the enthronement of God, the King, and the mystical Creator of all things, in his own Kingdom of Heaven; it is he who perfects the Maker of all things! In certain spheres of being, divine and human existence are intertwined. The intrinsic, extramundane process of *Tikkun*, symbolically described as the birth of God's personality, corresponds to the process of mundane history . . . and its innermost soul, [which] prepares the way for the final restitution of all the scattered and exiled lights and sparks. . . . Every act of man is related to this final task which God has set for his creatures." Scholem, *Major Trends*.

The advent of Our Lord Jesus Christ would be the special application, appropriate to our human species, of a hominal principle emanated by the Word from the beginning.[6] And if, as far as the past is concerned, the Christian dogma of the Incarnation and the doctrine of Adam Kadmon can be isolated from each other, it seems that, for the future, they are closely linked, because just as the king of the Kabbalah has the community of Israel as his bride, so Christ has the Church as his bride; and all the faithful, St Paul tells us, are members of a mystical body of which Christ is the head.[7]

[6] Original editor's note: In the author's original manuscript the following variant was found, which is of sufficient interest to reproduce here: "The advent of Our Lord Jesus Christ would be the special application to our human species of a metaphysical humanity invested by the Word from the beginning."

[7] "The true nature of redemption is therefore mystical, and its historical and national aspects are merely ancillary symptoms which constitute a visible symbol of its consummation. . . . It is here that we have the point where the mystical and the Messianic element in Luria's doctrine are welded together. The *Tikkun*, the path to the end of all things, is also the path to the beginning. Theosophic cosmology, the doctrine of the emergence of all things from God, becomes its opposite, the doctrine of Salvation as the return of all things to their original contact with God." Scholem, *Major Trends*.

www.ingramcontent.com/pod-product-compliance
Lightning Source LLC
Chambersburg PA
CBHW030844090426
42737CB00009B/1100